The Verbum Book
of Scanned Imagery

Also by Linnea Dayton and Michael Gosney
The Verbum Book of Electronic Page Design
M&T Books/Prentice Hall, 1990

The Verbum Book of PostScript Illustration
(with Janet Ashford)
M&T Books/Prentice Hall, 1990

The Verbum Book of Digital Painting
(with Paul Goethel)
M&T Books, 1990

The Verbum Book
of Scanned Imagery

Michael Gosney ▮ Linnea Dayton ▮ Phil Inje Chang

M&T BOOKS

M&T Books
A Division of M&T Publishing, Inc.
501 Galveston Drive
Redwood City, CA 94063

Printed in the United States of America
First Edition published 1991

Library of Congress Cataloging-in-Publication Data
Gosney, Michael, 1954–
    The verbum book of scanned imagery / Michael Gosney, Linnea Dayton, Phil Inje Chang. — 1st ed.
    p. cm. — (The Verbum electronic art and design series)
Includes index.
ISBN 1-55851-091-5: $29.95
    1. Computer art — Study and teaching.
    I. Dayton, Linnea, 1944–   II. Chang, Phil Inje.   III. Verbum (San Diego, Calif.)
    IV. Title.   V. Series
    N7433.G68 1990
    760- -dc20   90-25009
                                     CIP

94 93 92 91   4 3 2 1

Produced by The Gosney Company, Inc. and *Verbum* magazine
670 Seventh Avenue, Second Floor
San Diego, CA 92101
(619) 233-9977

Book and cover design: John Odam
Cover illustration: Jack Davis
Back cover illustrations: Lind Babcock, Jack Davis, Sharon Steuer, Greg Vander Houwen
Production Manager: Martha Siebert
Production Assistants: Jonathan Parker, Mike Swartzbeck
Administrative Manager: Jeanne Lear
Technical Graphics Consultant: Jack Davis
Proofreading, research: Valerie Bayla, Jackie Estrada

Contents

n this book you will find a remarkable new world. The *Verbum Book of Scanned Imagery* focuses on an exciting new kind of graphic art process: the use of video digitizing hardware and image retouching software to capture images from a variety of sources, manipulate them, and reproduce them in print or video forms. This pc-based technology has created a revolution in the printing field, allowing for digital creation, preparation and direct film output of halftones and color separations. But the really exciting fruit of scanned imagery technology, when it comes into the hands of adventuresome artists, is illustrative work. Inspired in part by the work of technically innovative illustrators such as Fred Otnes and painters such as Andy Warhol and Robert Rauschenberg, artists working with Macintosh, MS-DOS and Amiga systems are retouching, manipulating and combining images with tools that represent one of the pc's most innovative contributions to the world of image making.

The *Verbum Book of Scanned Imagery,* like the other books in the Verbum Electronic Art and Design Series, is an art instruction book, rather than a technical computer book. The first two chapters of the book will give you an overview of scanning and image retouching technology and the personal computer products that make it possible. The following chapters take you through the step-by-step development of projects by talented artists. Each chapter introduces the artist and project, and re-creates both the technical steps and the artist's creative thought processes as the project was

JACK DAVIS

developed. At the end of most chapters is a Portfolio of other scanned imagery examples by the artist, with brief descriptions of each.

You'll find sidebars and tips throughout the book. The sidebars provide supportive information on significant subjects. ▌ *Tips are introduced by this vertical symbol, and they appear in italics.*

An extensive Gallery of exemplary illustrative works follows the project chapters. These samples are from artists who have had extensive experience with personal computer design systems. We've chosen works that represent effective and innovative use of the electronic retouching and painting tools. At the end of the book, a Glossary provides terms and definitions, and an Appendix lists useful products and services. Production Notes provide details on the development of the book itself. And, of course, the Index will help you find specific information.

Origins of scanned imagery

Scanning has been a part of computer technology since the early mainframes, but it wasn't popularized until economical systems for use with personal computers emerged in the mid-1980s. The original Macintosh encouraged the use of scanned imagery with its accommodation of bitmapped images, and inexpensive third-party products such as ThunderScan (which used a scanning module fitted in place of the ribbon cartridge in the Apple ImageWriter printer) and MacVision, an interface box that digitized any video source into the Mac. The Amiga brought full-color video digitizing into popular use with low-cost hardware systems.

Artists used scanners to bring images into publications as low-resolution halftones and to incorporate them into illustrative works, creating an exciting new art form we've called "electronic montage." The use of scanned imagery by illustrators was accelerated with the introduction of the PostScript drawing program Adobe Illustrator, which accepted a scanned image "template" for tracing. As desktop publishing software advanced in capability and high-resolution scanners improved, the world of desktop color separation emerged. Today, designers routinely scan black-and-white and color images, retouch them as necessary and output them directly to film as part of a page layout. Illustrators also use high-powered scanning systems increasingly for the kind of photo montage works featured in this book.

Video producers and photographers are increasingly aware of the personal computer's scanning capabilities. Still-video cameras that capture images electronically on magnetic disks (just as a video camera captures images on magnetic tape) provide electronic images that are easily digitized. "Digital photography" is a new specialty in the world of commercial and fine art photography, where photographers enhance and combine their photographs with the same pc tools used by illustrators and designers. Video input is becoming more widely used as pc systems are adapted for video editing and production of multimedia presentations.

On an established plateau

After several years of evolution, this scanning and digitizing hardware and image retouching software is well-established. A plateau has been reached. We now have hardware and software standards, support services and networks of artists using these tools. Most of the tools, even if on different hardware platforms, work in similar fashion. We don't anticipate quantum leaps during the next few years that will make the existing standards obsolete; rather we expect steady refinements of existing tools, added speed and power in hardware platforms, and progressive innovations in high-end processes such as scanning and color separation. That's why most of the material in this book will be useful to you regardless of your specific system configuration, and for several years to come.

What is Verbum?

Verbum, the Journal of Personal Computer Aesthetics, is a magazine dedicated to exploring the aesthetic and human aspects of using microcomputers. Founded in 1986 by a group of artists and writers who had the good fortune to be involved with the early electronic design tools, the journal has tracked the evolution of electronic design and illustration tools, contributing the artist's perspective (and conscience) to an industry that has at times been unbalanced in its commercial and technical emphasis.

Each issue of *Verbum* has served as an example of the latest desktop publishing tools, beginning with the early issue's laser-printed camera-ready art on up to today's digital four-color separations. Through the development of the magazine, we've helped to galvanize the community of advanced artists, programmers and industry visionaries who have pushed the new frontier forward. As an ongoing experiment, *Verbum* has covered not only electronic design, but illustration, fine art, typography, digitized imaging, 3D graphics, animation, music and even the new realm of interactive multimedia. The Verbum Electronic Art and Design Series was conceived as a way to bring *Verbum's* accumulated resources into a practical, instructional context.

Beyond the magazine, Verbum has been involved in popularizing PC-assisted art as a fine art form. The Verbum team has produced the "Imagine" exhibit of personal computer art since the spring of 1988. Sponsored by Apple Computer, Inc., Letraset U.S.A., SuperMac Technology and other firms, Imagine has been an evolving exhibit featuring the work of over 60 artists from around the world. Major shows have been held in Boston, San Diego and Tokyo, with abbreviated exhibits at conferences in Toronto, Washington, D.C., San Francisco and Los Angeles. As of the fall of 1990, the Verbum Gallery of Digital Art is open in San Diego, showcasing some of the top digital painters from the United States and other countries.

A few acknowledgments

The Verbum Book of Scanned Imagery and the entire *Verbum* book series has involved the helpful efforts of many people, too many to mention here. But we would like to give special thanks to the contributing artists who committed that most precious resource to the project — time — and especially to Jack Davis for his technical review and illustrations. Also, we would like to thank our literary agent William Gladstone; our patient editor at M&T Books, Brenda McLaughlin; our service bureau here in San Diego, Central Graphics; and the many software and hardware companies who helped keep us up-to-date on products. Finally, we'd like to thank our *Verbum* readers, who keep inspiring us to push the envelope — just a little further!

CHAPTER 1

An Overview

Digitized imaging is the link that brings pictures from the outside world into the domain of the computer, where they can be displayed, changed (resized, reshaped or otherwise altered) and then reproduced on paper, film or videotape (Figure 1). The idea of bringing images from the real world into the computer is almost as old as computer graphics itself. Early systems based on large computers (mainframes or minicomputers) focused on specialized industrial applications, such as *OCR* (*optical character recognition*, which is reading text from printed pages), video effects and image manipulation (called *collage* or *montage*) and direct reproduction for print. Today, artists using personal computers can make creative use of any scrap of reality that can be digitized (Figure 2).

Figure 1. Digitized imaging. Jack Davis assembled this collage of digitized images on a Mac IIci with the Adobe Photoshop color image-editing program. Some of the elements are the artist's original 3D models created in Swivel 3D Professional with scanned textures and reflections built into them. Other elements are from the artist's personal "scrap collection" of materials digitized with a Sharp JX-450 flatbed scanner.

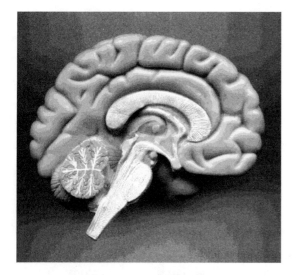

Figure 2. Creative scanning. Graphic designer John Odam used a flatbed scanner (an Apple Scanner) to scan these three-dimensional objects. A plastic model of a brain, to add depth to an anatomical diagram, was scanned with a piece of white foam-core board behind it, supported by shims. To achieve the black background for the light bulb, the scanner lid was left open. The scan was then reduced disproportionately (squeezed vertically) to make it look rounder than it really was. The scanned image of the coins was made with the scanner lid closed. Advance planning and the ability to rotate a scanned image in an image-editing program can lead to good use of the shadows that occur in scanning even thin three-dimensional objects.

Input

Scanned, or digitized, imagery involves four processes: input, display, manipulation and output. *Input* means converting the visual information in an image into numbers, the kind of information that the computer can handle. In desktop systems, this can involve scanning flat or three-dimensional objects, photographic prints, slides or transparencies; video capture via a video camera, videocassette recorder (VCR) or videodisc player and a video capture device in the computer that can interpret the video signal and convert it to digital information; or recording with a still video device that acts like a normal camera but stores its snapshots on disk. Digitized images can then be stored on electromagnetic media such as floppy disks or hard disks or on optical media such as CD ROM (read-only memory on compact disk) (Figure 3).

How a scanner works To get the best results from the scanning process, you need to understand a bit about how the technology works. Scanning an

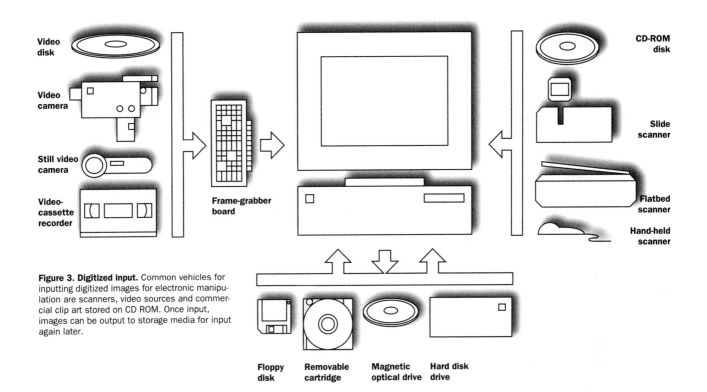

Figure 3. Digitized input. Common vehicles for inputting digitized images for electronic manipulation are scanners, video sources and commercial clip art stored on CD ROM. Once input, images can be output to storage media for input again later.

image involves training an optical sensing device on an object (such as a photograph) one "strip" at a time, in order to read and record its image. The scan is recorded as a field of tiny samples, and each sample is then represented electronically as a dot of black or white, some intensity of gray or a color. The optical sensing device is operated by a software program — a set of directions the computerized scanning mechanism can understand.

A *scanner* bounces light off (or passes light through) a narrow strip of an image or object. The light, which has been changed by being reflected from (or by travelling through) the strip, is directed to an assembly of detecting devices called a CCD (charge-coupled device) array. Each CCD is electrically charged by the light from one tiny area of the scanned strip, and that charge is proportional to the amount of light that hits that particular CCD. An analog-to-digital (A/D) converter translates the electrical charge registered by each CCD into digital information — a number that can be processed and stored by the computer (Figure 4).

After numbers have been recorded for all the tiny areas of a strip, the scanner's sensing device records information from the next stripe. The scanning process is repeated until the whole image has been digitized. The result is a set of numbers that represents the levels of light and dark (or colors) in all the areas of the scanned object.

Scanners vary not only in the way they use light (by bouncing it off a reflective subject such as a piece of paper, or by passing it through a 35mm slide, for example), but also in resolution (how many tiny samples the scanner takes in a given area), the number of colors and levels of light they can

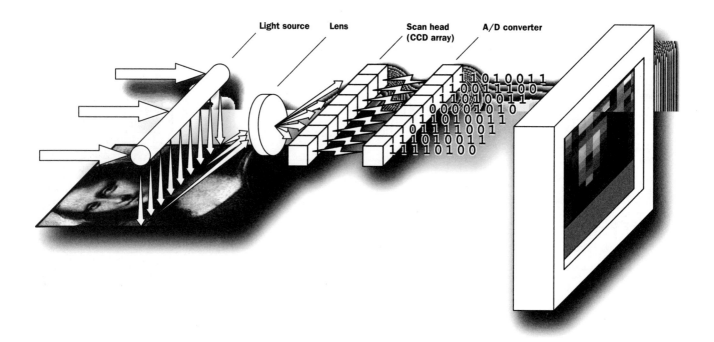

Light source   Lens   Scan head (CCD array)   A/D converter

distinguish (a full range of colors; black, white and levels of gray; or black and white only) and how much their software can do to correct and change the scanned image.

Resolution Scanner input resolution is usually measured in dots per inch or *dpi* (see "Input terminology" on page 5). Resolution is determined by the number of CCDs per inch that are available to receive the light from the scanned object. Usually this is the same as the number of strips per inch. Adding CCDs and engineering them to fit more densely increases the cost of the scanner.

Up to a point, the higher the density of CCDs, the better the image that can be created by the scanner. However, if the input resolution is much higher than the resolution at which the image will be output, the extra input resolution is wasted. The wasted input resolution has a cost attached to it, too, since each input dot takes up space in the computer's working memory (*random access memory,* or *RAM*) as well as disk storage space (Figure 5).

Black-and-white, grays and color The highest number of levels (intensities or densities) of gray the scanner can produce depends on the highest setting available for the A/D converters. If the A/D converters divide the voltage readings from the CCDs into two levels, the result is a black-and-white bitmap. Black-and-white bitmaps are also known as 1-bit scans because only 1 bit is required to store the "presence" or "absence" of a dot at each dot location in the image (Figure 6). One-bit scans are often used for scanning line art to be reduced and printed or to be used as a template for drawing in a PostScript illustration program (see "Scanning line art " on page 9). Used this way, a 1-bit scanning process sets a threshold (brightness level) for deciding whether a line is present (black) or absent (white) (Figure 7). The scanning

Figure 4. How a scanner works. In a flatbed scanner a focusing lens directs light reflected from the scanned object to an array of charge-coupled devices (CCDs), which convert the light to electrical charges. An analog-to-digital (A/D) converter transforms the voltages from the CCDs to numbers the computer can store and use for display and printing. In the example diagrammed here, an 8-bit number (any number from 0 to 255) can be stored for each dot. This provides a range of 256 potential grays that can be specified for each dot.

Original image, printed here as a halftone

CRAIG McCLAIN

37.5 dpi, 11k

75 dpi, 39k

Figure 5. Scanning resolution and file size. Increasing the number of samples per inch the scanner records increases the amount of information to be stored. Each doubling of the scanning resolution approximately quadruples file size.

150 dpi, 154k

300 dpi, 613k

Input resolution terminology

Scanner input resolution is typically described in terms of *dots per inch (dpi)*. Dpi is a measure of dots per linear distance, not dots per area. So 300 dpi, for example, means that if you looked very closely at a single line of dots recorded by a scanner, you would see 300 of them lined up over the distance of 1 inch. Three hundred of these lines of dots, stacked up, would form a square composed of 300 x 300, or 90,000 dots per square inch.

Sometimes different terminology is used to define resolution. Instead of dpi, input resolution is described in terms of *lines*. For example, resolution may be described as *2000 lines*, or sometimes even *2K lines*. Using the term *lines* can cause confusion since the same terminology is used in describing the halftone screens used for output. And using *K* to mean *thousand* can be confusing because this terminology is most commonly used to describe file size and memory requirements. Although scan resolution is related to both the halftone screen frequency you might choose for output and the amount of memory a scanned image file occupies, the relationship is not direct, and so the "shared" terminology can be confusing.

process doesn't distinguish gray levels between black and white. When a 1-bit scanner is used in *dithered* rather than line-art mode, grays are represented by dot patterns (Figure 8).

If voltage readings are divided into 4, 8, 16 or more levels, that number of grays will be available to characterize each dot. The more gray levels, of course, the more subtle the gradations possible in the final image — that is, the more it will look like a traditional continuous-tone photograph (Figure 9). An upper limit of 256 levels of gray makes sense because it provides more grays than the unaided human eye can distinguish and because 256 levels is the maximum amount of information that can be stored in one computer byte (8 bits) (refer to Figure 6).

Three times as much information is picked up in a 24-bit color scan as in a full grayscale scan (Figure 10). The CCDs measure the intensity of each of the three primary colors of light — red, green and blue (RGB) — and thus three bytes of data are needed for each dot. This makes a color scan file very large compared to a grayscale image (refer to Figure 6; see "Calculating storage requirements" on page 7).

Color scanners vary in their *dynamic range,* a measure of the part of the entire visible spectrum that's captured in a scan. The larger a scanner's dynamic range, the more likely it is to produce a scan whose colors are true to those of the original scanned subject.

1-bit	2^1	2 shades (B&W)	
2-bit	2^2	4 shades	
4-bit	2^4	16 shades	
8-bit	2^8	256 shades	
16-bit	2^{16}	65,536 shades	
24-bit	2^{24}	16,777,216 shades	

Figure 6. Bits and shades. In the binary number system on which computer operations are based, a 1-bit scan produces 2^1 (or 2) different shades — black and white only. A 4-bit scan provides 2^4 (or 16) shades, and so on. One byte can store 8 bits of information, or 256 shades.

1-bit, 18k

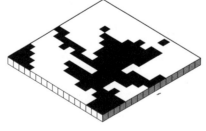

Figure 7. 1-bit scans. A black-and-white scanned image is considered to be only 1 bit "deep," because all the information ("on" or "off," black or white, 0 or 1) to describe each of the dots in the image can be stored in a 1-bit number.

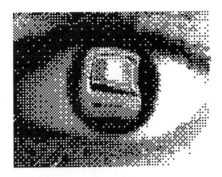

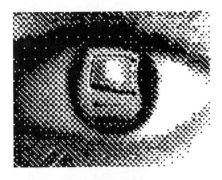

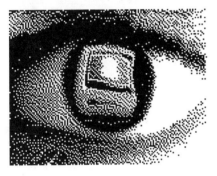

Figure 8. Dithering. A 1-bit scanner can be used in a dithering mode to represent levels of gray between black and white. Patterns of black and white dots are used to represent gray areas. Patterns shown here are at 72 dpi.

Adjusting and modifying the scanned image Once the scan data is collected and stored (or in some cases during the scanning process itself), the image can be adjusted — for example, to change the brightness (the overall lightness or darkness of an image), the contrast (the difference between the lightest and darkest parts of an image) or gamma (the level of contrast in midtones of the image). In general, and especially with color scans, it's advantageous to adjust brightness, contrast and gamma at the time of the scan, since this is the time when information is being recorded. If you leave these adjustments until after the scan is saved, you may find that you haven't recorded the information you need to make the changes you want.

Some scanner software also allows cropping, scaling and other changes to the image. Other scanner programs are limited in their adjustment functions, leaving further modification to image-editing software designed specifically for that purpose.

Calibration Good scanners run calibration tests before a scan, to find and fix any variations in the way the CCDs are responding to light. Variations occur because the individual CCDs put out slightly different amounts of voltage in response to light. This variability, a result of normal manufacturing processes, can be compounded by changes in temperature or by the wear that occurs with use. Calibration software compares a scanner's current readings to a standard scale and then adjusts for any variance it finds.

Storage formats To be useful, a scanned image has to be stored in a format that can be read by the computer and the software you work with. Most grayscale and color scanners save images as TIFF (tagged image file format) files. Some also save them in PICT, EPS (encapsulated PostScript) or MacPaint formats (see "File formats" on page 11). In addition, some image-editing programs that have their own scanner *drivers*, software that operates the scanner, save scanned images in their own format.

Calculating storage requirements

The amount of storage space needed to hold a scanned image depends on the resolution (dots per inch, or dpi), the size of the original scanned artwork (number of inches) and the number of bits the scanner uses to record the information for each dot. The formula for calculating about how much room you'll need to store a scanned image can be expressed as shown in the equation below.

Keep in mind that the amount of working memory needed to modify a scanned image can be more than the storage size, because until a modified version of the scan is saved, the computer has to have room to maintain both the original image and the modifications. However, some of the image-editing software used to modify scanned images has built-in file compression, which reduces the amount of memory needed to store the file.

$$\frac{dpi^2 \times \text{bits per dot} \times \text{width of image} \times \text{height of image}}{8 \text{ (the number of bits per byte)} \times 1024 \text{ (the number of bytes per kilobyte)}} = \text{kilobytes}$$

Display

After data is collected and saved in a scan, it can be used to display the scanned image on the screen of a computer monitor. Regardless of how much grayscale or color data is stored in a scan, a black-and-white monitor can display only a black-and-white bitmapped version of the image. A grayscale monitor can display 256 different brightnesses (or levels of gray). A full-color RGB monitor can display 24 bits of color information for each dot on the screen, or over 16.7 million colors including a full range of grays (refer to Figure 6).

A second kind of color display, using 8 bits of information for each on-screen dot, displays color with a smaller number of colors visible on the screen at a time. In the case of a 24-bit color scan displayed on an 8-bit RGB monitor, all the information that would be used to display a full-color image on a 24-bit monitor is available to the computer, but the 8-bit monitor can display only 256 of the colors at once. So an *indexed lookup table* is built that stores

8-bit, 105k

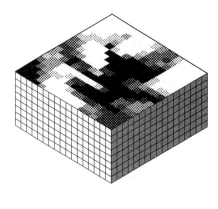

Figure 9. Grayscale scans. A full grayscale scanned image is considered to be 8 bits deep, because in order to store the information to describe 256 levels of gray, 8 bits of information must be stored for each dot.

24-bit, 329k

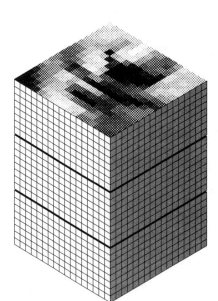

Figure 10. Full-color scans. A full-color scan is 24 bits deep. That is, the scanner registers 24 bits of information for each dot. Each of the three additive primary colors (red, green and blue) requires 8 bits of information to store a number between 0 and 255, for a total of 24 bits for the three colors.

Scanning line art

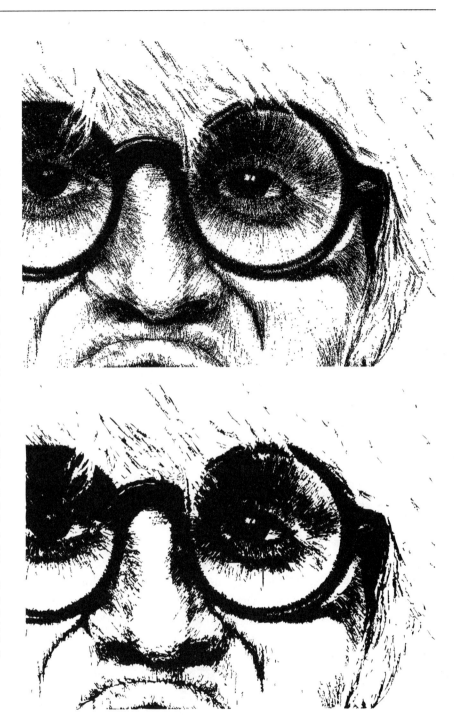

Scanning in 1-bit-per-pixel line-art mode has its limitations. Although line-art scans at high resolution (300 dots per inch, for example) are useful for optical character recognition (OCR) tasks, where the clarity of the letters is crucial, scans of black-and-white art are somewhat limited in usefulness. A 300 dpi bitmap can take up a lot more storage and computer working space than an equivalent PostScript illustration, for example, in which the drawing is stored as a series of objects defined mathematically rather than by mapping the position of each dot, so that it can be output at the highest resolution the printer or other output device is capable of. Bitmaps can also cause long delays in printing on PostScript printers.

A bitmapped illustration can often be successfully scaled down (reduced in size before printing), which effectively increases the resolution by packing in more dots per inch. But it can't be sized up without emphasizing its pixelated nature. Magnification produces a stairstepped effect. Even without magnification, unless lines are perfectly straight and either horizontal or vertical, they suffer from the "jaggies." And unlike PostScript drawings, increasing output resolution doesn't improve the bitmapped appearance beyond the resolution of the original scan. One way to take advantage of scanning and still produce smooth lines and curves is to import the bitmap into a program like Illustrator, FreeHand, Streamline or Corel Draw, where it can be autotraced (or even traced by hand) to convert it to PostScript lines.

The image at the top is scanned line art by San Diego artist Stephen King saved as a 1-bit TIFF. At the bottom is a Streamline autotracing of the bitmap. The tracing retains much of the sketchlike quality of the bitmap, but can be resized without losing its definition.

the information for each of 256 colors that, when used on-screen, will produce the closest possible match for the full-color image. By zooming in on a small area of a color image and thereby narrowing the range of colors to be displayed to 256 or fewer, it's possible to see true 24-bit color for that small area. Many color scanners offer the option of saving a scan in 8-bit rather than 24-bit color, for use with an 8-bit monitor or with software limited to 256 colors, where the extra color information wouldn't be useful.

The resolution (dots per inch) of the screen display of a scan depends on the resolution built into the screen itself. Macintosh monitors, for instance, typically have a resolution of 72 dpi. So a scan recorded at 150 dpi will be displayed on a Mac screen at approximately double its original dimensions — each dot recorded in the scan will take up not 1/150 inch, but 1/72 inch, so about twice as many linear inches (or four times as much area) will be needed.

Manipulation

A variety of tools are available for editing black-and-white, grayscale and color images, either to clean them up or to transform them from realistic pictures to artworks. Black-and-white bitmaps can be altered by using the tools available in painting programs to change individual black dots to white or vice versa (Figure 11). Grayscale and color image-editing programs provide ways to vary brightness, contrast and gamma. Many can also do some very sophisticated painting — imitating airbrush and watercolor effects, for example (Figure 12) — and can add special effects to images (Figure 13). Many also allow *masking*, isolating a part of an image so it can be changed (or protected from change) independently of the rest of the image (Figure 14).

Besides editing pictures, many image-editing programs are ideal for changing file formats. Image editors were designed to work on scans that might be imported in MacPaint, TIFF, PICT or some other format and would need to be exported in a form that a page layout or other program could use. So they can import and export many file types. Even if you don't want to change the way a picture looks, an image editor can be handy for changing its file type so it can be passed between two programs that don't share a common file format.

Figure 11. Modifying 1-bit scans. Black-and-white scans can be edited with painting software. Many of the white areas in this 1-bit scan were filled with different densities of a black-and-white dot pattern in Photoshop.

Figure 12. "Painting" with image editors. Many color or gray-scale image-editing programs include tools for producing artwork that imitates traditional drawing and painting tools. Watercolor and airbrush can be simulated in most image-editing software. This "charcoal" drawing by Jack Davis was done with Photoshop's paintbrush tool and a Wacom digitizing tablet.

File formats

The first Mac and IBM PC graphics programs, like MacPaint and PC Paintbrush, saved files in their own native formats. Since screen resolution on the Mac is a standard 72 dpi, MacPaint format (also at 72 dpi) became the standard file format for single-bit (black-and-white), low-resolution bitmaps on the Mac. Desktop scanners, even though they offered higher resolutions, provided an option to save in this format (or similar ones on the PC) because these images could be edited so easily with existing software.

Another early graphics file format choice was PICT, Apple's original interprogram-transferrable file type that defined lines and shapes as a series of equations rather than a collection of individual dot descriptions. The PICT format was designed to be a standard for exporting and importing graphics, so they could be passed from one program to another. The PICT format also has the capacity to accommodate bitmaps.

When it became apparent that scanned files would become important in the desktop market, Aldus Corporation introduced a more flexible and sophisticated format for storing scans. *TIFF,* or *tagged image file format,* accommodates files with several bits of scanned information per dot and allows programs that import such files to extract the information they need for display or editing. The implementation of Color QuickDraw on the Mac and VGA on the PC made it possible to display grayscale images — often in TIFF format — with photographic realism.

But one of the main advantages of TIFF is also its main drawback. Its flexibility means that many software developers can support it, but it also means that it's open to interpretation. As a consequence, there are many versions of TIFF.

Other file formats for scanned images include PICT2 and encapsulated PostScript (EPS, or EPSF). In PICT2 the ability to carry color or grayscale information has been added to the PICT file format. EPS files include a PICT preview for screen display along with a PostScript description of the file. EPS tends to take more disk space than other formats.

Figure 13. Using special effects. Several special-effects "filters" from Adobe Photoshop were used to produce these light bulbs. Clockwise from upper left are the unaltered scanned image, Ripple, Add Noise, Sphere, Pinch and Find Edges. In some cases, the filters were applied several times to the image to produce the desired effect.

Output

Output is producing the image in a form that can be reproduced — for example, on slide film, videotape or paper. The most common way to output scanned images to be printed on paper is to produce a positive or negative image on paper or film and then transfer it to a printing plate to run on a press. In output, as in scanning, resolution is important. To achieve the best output quality, it's important to have the right relationship between the scan resolution and the printed resolution (see "Resolution in scanning, display and output" on page 14).

Black-and-white 1-bit scans can be successfully output on many computerized printers. Since these bitmaps have usually been scanned at fairly low resolution, nothing is lost if low-resolution output is used — and likewise nothing is gained by increasing the resolution of the output beyond that of the original scan (Figure 15). But with a grayscale image, a big change is needed to transform the information stored in the scan and displayed as various intensities of light on a grayscale monitor into an ink-on-paper print. This transformation is usually accomplished with *halftone screens.* The screens are formed of rows of *cells,* and each cell can hold a halftone dot. Various shades of gray are formed by using larger or smaller halftone dots within the cells (Figure 16). Because the first printers' screens were made by etching lines in glass to form a screen pattern when light was shined through them, screen

Figure 14. Masking. In this Photoshop image the figure was selected and masked to protect it during painting of the background with the Impressionist setting of the rubber stamp tool. The "halo" effect around the figure was created with the airbrush.

densities (the number of rows of cells in a given distance) are usually described in terms of *lines per inch (lpi)*.

In digital printers and imagesetters (high-resolution output devices that produce images on either paper or film) the dots that fill the cells are made up of smaller, square dots — the number of these smaller dots depends on the imagesetter's resolution (see "Resolution in scanning, display and output" on page 14). Typically, when the resolution is higher, the number of grays available for printing is greater, and the printed image is smoother and more like the continuous tone of a traditional photograph.

Resolution in scanning, display and output

To achieve the best quality when you print images that incorporate scans, it's important to have the right relationship between the scan resolution and the resolution of the halftone screen used for output. Resolution of the scan is also important at the photo-manipulation stage between input and output because it determines the size of the image on-screen and the storage size of the file.

Input resolution, usually expressed in dots per inch (dpi), determines how much information is picked up from the original image and stored. Failure to store enough information can lead to disappointment later because there's no way, short of starting over with a new scan, to add the information needed to maintain the sharpness of the image for reproduction. However, the more information in the scan, the bigger the file and the longer the wait for screen refresh, scrolling and so forth during the editing process. So it's important to know, before you scan, what resolution to use to get as much information as you need, but not much extra.

On-screen resolution is hardware-limited. On standard Macintosh displays, for example, screen resolution is 72 dpi. When a scanned image is opened on the Mac for display on-screen, each dot in the original scan takes up a $1/72$ x $1/72$-inch space. That means that if the original was a scan of a 35mm slide at 2000 dots per inch, the image would occupy about 26 x 38 inches on-screen. Obviously, to have control of the individual pixels during the editing of the image, you'd have to work on only part of the image at a time, because only part would fit on the screen. Although you can resize or resample an image within a photo-manipulation program to make it smaller and easier to work with, you risk losing image quality.

Halftone screen resolution of the printed piece, expressed in screen lines per inch (lpi), determines how much of the

information from the original scan will be useful in the final output of the image. Most photographic images are printed at resolutions of 120, 133 or 150 lpi on press. To get a good-quality print from a scanned image, there should be at least 1 dot per inch of scan resolution for each line per inch of the halftone screen so that the program that applies the screen to the image doesn't have to create information to put in some of the halftone cells. More than 1 scan dot of information per cell can be useful; the program can "average" the information from 2 or more dots before assigning characteristics to a cell. Theoretically, the more information, the better the average that the program will arrive at. But in practical terms, almost no image quality is gained beyond a 2:1 ratio of scan information to printed halftone resolution. Even the difference between 1:1 and 2:1 can be insignificant for some images, especially those with organic, curved shapes. The higher ratio becomes important, however, in reproduction of photo images with straight lines. Those lines at an angle just off horizontal or vertical tend to show a "stairstepping" effect at the lower ratio that becomes less obvious as the program averages grayscale or color information at higher ratios to provide antialiasing.

An example
Here's a good way to determine the scan resolution you should use for a color image that will eventually be printed with a halftone screen, in a magazine, for example:
• First, determine how many dots per inch you'll need in order to provide between 1 and 2 dots per halftone cell. To do this, you'll need to know the halftone screen frequency and the final printed size of the piece. In this example, the screen frequency is 150 lpi and the critical factor in the final printed size is a width of 5 inches (**a**).
• Multiply the screen frequency by the size to get the minimum number of dots (or pixels) wide that the image should be.

Then double this figure to provide a 2:1 ratio between input dots and output cells. Remember that the 2:1 ratio may be more than you need; 1.25:1 works well in many instances. In this case, 150 x 5 = 750 pixels; 2 x 750 = 1500 pixels.
• Next, calculate the scan resolution necessary to get this number of dots from the width of the 35mm slide. The slide's image area measures $1\frac{3}{8}$ (or 1.375) inches wide. Dividing the 1500 pixels by 1.375 gives the number of dots per inch needed in scanning: $1500 \div 1.375 = 1090$ dpi (**b**). Set the slide scanner close to this setting.
• The vertical dimension of the 1500-pixel-wide image can be calculated from the height of the image area of the 35mm slide, which is $\frac{15}{16}$ (or .9375) inch: $1500 \div 1.375 = X \div .9375$; $X = 1090 \times .9375 \approx 1022$ dots. So a screen image at the standard resolution of 72 dpi would be about 21 inches wide by 14 inches high; that is, $1500 \div 72 \approx 21$ and $1022 \div 72 \approx 14$ (**c**).
• If the scan is a 24-bit color scan, the file would occupy about 4.6 MB of memory: Each of the three colors (red, green and blue) requires 8 bits (or 1 byte) of storage for each dot in the image; so for all three colors, 3 bytes per dot are required. The total number of dots in the image is $1500 \times 1022 = 1,533,000$ dots. So the storage capacity required is approximately $1,533,000 \times 3 = 4,599,000$ bytes, or 4.6 MB. If your scanner doesn't scan directly to hard disk, but instead stores the scan in RAM as it's being made, you'll need at least 4.6 MB of RAM free to make the scan.
• Note that if you started with a glossy print of the image instead of a 35mm slide and scanned it on a flatbed scanner with a resolution of 400 dpi, to get the same resolution in the final print, you would need to start with a print $3\frac{3}{4}$ (or 3.75) inches wide; that is, 1500 dots $\div$ 400 dots per inch = 3.75 inches (**d**).

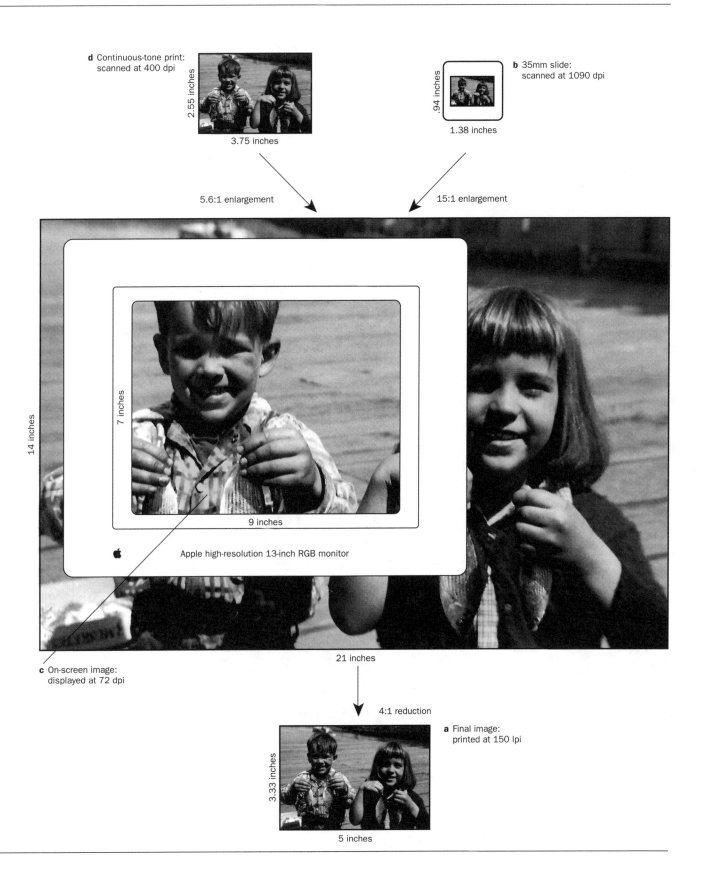

d Continuous-tone print:
scanned at 400 dpi

2.55 inches

3.75 inches

b 35mm slide:
scanned at 1090 dpi

.94 inches

1.38 inches

5.6:1 enlargement

15:1 enlargement

14 inches

7 inches

9 inches

Apple high-resolution 13-inch RGB monitor

21 inches

c On-screen image:
displayed at 72 dpi

4:1 reduction

3.33 inches

5 inches

a Final image:
printed at 150 lpi

Color separation To print a color scanned image, several transformations have to take place between the scanner or monitor and the printed page. First, the RGB color information used by the scanner and the display monitor has to be translated into a different color system — the one used for inks in the printing process. This system is called CMYK (for cyan, magenta, yellow and black). Just as red, green and blue are the primary colors of light, cyan, magenta, yellow and black are the primary colors of printing inks, which when "mixed" provide the entire printed spectrum (see "Color systems" on page 19). Process colors are mixed by printing different amounts of the four primaries on top of one another. Once the color scan information is translated into CMYK percentages, the data for each color has to be separated out so that the four process colors can be printed in turn, overlaying one another in different densities to form all the colors of the image. Usually a halftone screen is produced for each of the four printing colors. (Not all electronic printing

Figure 15. Scanning and output resolution. The resolution of a scan saved at a resolution of 72 dpi is not improved by increasing the output resolution to 300 dpi (left) or 1270 dpi (middle). However, reducing a 72 dpi scan before outputting it can increase the apparent resolution of the image. The image on the right was scanned at twice the size shown here and reduced before output at 1270 dpi.

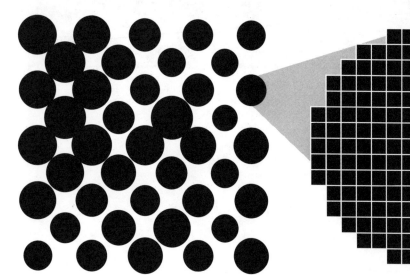

Figure 16. Halftoning. Electronically created halftone screens are used to represent shades of gray. Halftone dots of various sizes are composed of smaller dots of uniform size.

processes use this separation process; other processes are described for individual models of color printers in Chapter 2).

So that the dots placed by the screens will visually blend to look like mixed colors, screens of the four process colors are printed at different angles (Figure 17). With the traditional printing methods used before digital color separations were possible, screens could be physically rotated into place so that these angles could be maintained exactly, as could the roundness of the halftone dots. In PostScript output devices, computer code written in the PostScript language tells the printer how to lay down the dots to form each angled screen. The screen density that can be supported, the roundness of the halftone dots and the ability to match the traditional printing angles all depend in part on the resolution of the output device. When PostScript halftone screens are used, high-resolution output (for example, at 2400 or 2540 dpi with a halftone screen of 150 lpi) produces the best results for both grayscale and color-separated images. And at this high resolution, output to film is preferable to paper output because of the small dot size. It's critical when you're dealing with these small dots to get from output to printing plate with the fewest possible steps, because at each step the photographic process can distort the dots (Figure 18). From negative to printing plate is a single step, but paper output requires two steps — from paper to film and then from film to plate.

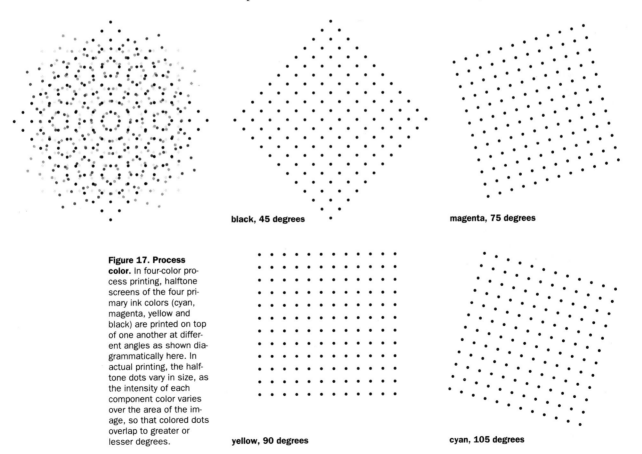

Figure 17. Process color. In four-color process printing, halftone screens of the four primary ink colors (cyan, magenta, yellow and black) are printed on top of one another at different angles as shown diagrammatically here. In actual printing, the halftone dots vary in size, as the intensity of each component color varies over the area of the image, so that colored dots overlap to greater or lesser degrees.

black, 45 degrees

magenta, 75 degrees

yellow, 90 degrees

cyan, 105 degrees

Figure 18. Output to film. Reproduction of grayscale and color scanned images requires high-resolution imagesetter output in order to print all the information stored in the image. Output to film (left) ensures better reproduction of the halftone dots that make up the image. If paper output is used (right), the image can become "muddy" as dots are distorted in rephotographing the image to make film before making the printing plate.

**Linotonic imagesetter output
to negative at 2540 dpi**

**Linotronic imagesetter output
to RC paper at 2540 dpi**

Video

Understanding the desktop interface with video can be a bit confusing, partly because video signals can take so many forms. The general concept of interfacing video and desktop computers can be explored by looking at the way NTSC (for National Television System Committee) format and the Apple video card (which drives the Mac's color monitors) interact.

NTSC is the most common video format — the one used in American TV sets for years. It's basically an *interlaced composite video signal with a scan rate of 30 Hz (hertz)*. This means that the typical TV picture is composed of two passes, or fields — one for even-numbered horizontal scan lines and one for odd-numbered scan lines. Each pass takes ⅟₆₀ second, so the whole frame takes ⅟₃₀ second to complete (30 Hz means 30 times per second). Because two scans interlock in this fashion, this kind of signal is called *interlaced*.

On a typical Mac II, however, an entire frame is completed in one pass in about ⅟₆₆ second. The video signal that drives the Mac's display monitor is *noninterlaced*, with a scan rate of 66.7 Hz. Besides these differences, the image information is packaged differently in the two systems. NTSC lumps all color, brightness and timing information in one *composite* signal, while the Mac separates RGB and timing components. It's possible to use these separate components and interlace them at TV scan rates. The result is an interlaced RGB signal at 30 Hz.

If a video capture board (the device that translates an outside video signal to a format the computer can use) is going to grab an NTSC signal directly, it has to do quite a bit of work to get decent results. Capturing and converting an NTSC signal involves two steps. The first step is *decoding* the composite signal into separate RGB and timing components. The second is *scan converting* the resulting RGB interlaced signal into a noninterlaced signal with the higher scan rate of the Mac. To export a video signal from computer to NTSC format, the conversion process is carried out in reverse.

Trends

Graphic design may demand high-precision screen frequencies, angles and dots of various shapes, and video editing may require scan-line conversion and NTSC output, but all this emphasis on the technical aspects of scanned imagery processes ignores a very important aspect of the technology's potential — creative vision. Photographs, the basis of much of desktop digitized imagery, have always been subject to manipulation. For as long as photographic negatives have existed, photographers and others have been applying darkroom magic — combining images and using retouching tools from the paintbrush to the airbrush. With expensive computerized scanning, color correcting and retouching systems like those of Scitex, Hell Graphics and Crosfield, the "seams" that resulted from such manipulations became less visible. But it wasn't until the ability to digitize a photo and modify it evolved on the desktop that the control of photo modifications was put back into the hands of the photographer. A photographer can now take a photo, transform it into an image on the computer screen and play with it, greatly extending the capabilities the darkroom/studio used to provide. Whether for commercial purposes or personal satisfaction, the creative use of any technology is the first step toward its assimilation in our daily lives.

Color systems

There are several systems of defining color, depending on how the color is produced or perceived. Four of the most common systems used in color image-editing and other graphics software are (1) RGB (red, green, blue), the additive color system; (2) HSL (hue, saturation, lightness), analogous to the way people perceive color; (3) PMS (the Pantone Matching System for defining color) and (4) CMYK (cyan, magenta, yellow, black), the subtractive color system, used for four-color process printing.

In the **RGB** system, used in video technology, various brightnesses of red, green and blue light combine to form the colors of the spectrum. On a television screen or computer monitor, the RGB color is created by light emitted from red, green and blue phosphors that coat the back of the screen and emit light when excited by an electron beam. The kind of color blending that results is similar to the process of combining spotlights on a stage. When full-strength red, green and blue are com-

bined, white light results; combinations of the three colors at less than full strength produce the other colors of the visible spectrum. One of the surprises in this system is that red and green combine to make yellow.

In the **HSL** system, color is defined by its hue (which depends on the wavelengths of light that are present), saturation (the purity of a color, determined by the number of different wavelengths present) and lightness (the brightness of the light, which depends on the amplitude of the light waves).

The **Pantone Matching System (PMS)** provides a standard for reproduction of colors with a system of premixed inks. Printed color swatches are assigned identification numbers. Several computer graphics programs have built-in or add-on PMS color selections that specify screen and four-color process equivalents of the Pantone colors for use in design and printing. Because Pantone colors are specified as spot colors, they don't play a big role in

editing the continuous-tone photos reproduced in scanned imagery.

The **CMYK** system is a subtractive color system, in which the colors of the visible spectrum are mixed by overlaying various densities of cyan, magenta, yellow and black inks, usually in very fine patterns of extremely small dots. These patterns are called halftone screens. The system is called subtractive because the printed inks absorb (subtract) certain wavelengths of the white light that hits them, reflecting the color that remains. For example, pure yellow ink reflects only specific yellow wavelengths, absorbing the others. As cyan, magenta and yellow are combined in increasing intensities, more wavelengths are absorbed and fewer are reflected, so that at full intensity they produce black. However, because of the nature of the inks and the way the colors overlay one another, the black produced this way can appear "muddy." Black ink is added or substituted to sharpen the dark colors.

CHAPTER 2

Hardware and Software

Perhaps more than any other computer-based design or illustration medium that artists and graphic designers use (such as PostScript-based illustration, electronic page design or digital painting), scanned imagery requires specific peripheral hardware. While electronic line drawing requires a computer and a drawing program, producing drawings doesn't require much equipment beyond the microcomputer, a monitor, a hard disk and a proofing printer. But using scanned imagery greatly expands the equipment involved in input and handling of the images.

Scanners

Digitizing hardware (primarily scanners and video digitizers) is to digitized imagery as the camera is to traditional photography. It provides the means for getting images into a system where they can be modified and output, as photographs are modified and output in the darkroom. Photographers choose different camera equipment depending on (1) what the subject is (large-format cameras are appropriate for panoramas of mountains, for example, but not necessarily for capturing the natural actions of small children), (2) what kind of image quality is needed for the way the photograph will be used (a photo for a full-color coffee-table book about the natural wonders of the western United States requires a different lens and film setup than one for a black-and-white daily newspaper), (3) how much automatic (versus manual) control the photographer wants the camera to have (should it adjust focus, shutter speed and lens opening automatically, or does the photographer want control of some or all of these things to personally control the range of effects that can be produced?) and (4) what the photographer can afford to pay for equipment and supplies.

Very similar choices have to be made in selecting input equipment for scanned imagery: Scanners come in several varieties, and the kind you need depends on several factors: What kinds of originals will you be scanning — three-dimensional, two-dimensional reflective (paper) or two-dimensional transparent (slides, for example)?

Do you want grayscale images (and if so, how many shades of gray) or full color? (Unlike the analogous camera, which lets you change film relatively easily depending on whether you want to record color or black-and-white, high contrast or a full range of intermediate grays choosing a grayscale scanner pretty much limits you to working without color, except for adding it through a colorizing process later.) And choosing a 16-level rather than a 256-level grayscale scanner limits your ability to simulate photographic results. Also, among color scanners there are different methods of recording color. Some color scanners record information for all three primary additive colors (red, green and blue) in a single pass of the scanning mechanism. Others make three passes, using filters in front of the lens to record only one color component on each pass. Images from three-pass systems tend to be less sharp than those from one-pass systems because of the error introduced by making and combining three separate scans.

What kind of resolution will you need to reproduce the scanned image in the medium and size you plan on (that is, how many dots per inch of information do you need to record)? ∎ *Although people often look at the high side of the resolution range, low resolution can be important also. For example, in scanning an original that is already halftoned, a resolution as low as 50 dpi can be helpful in avoiding moirés, interference patterns that can appear in scanned or printed images.*

And, given a resolution, how important are the fine points of image quality — can you live with the equivalent of a drugstore camera or do you need a Haselbladt, or something in between? How much do you want the software that comes with the scanner to be able to do in terms of cropping an image, adjusting contrast and brightness or "retouching" the image, and how much of this are you willing to defer to the "darkroom" of the separate image-editing software? (Figure 1) Is a prescan feature important, so you can get a quick on-screen image to check crop and alignment so you can make adjustments if necessary before starting the full scan? Do you need a scanner that scans to disk (saves the scanned image to a hard disk as it scans) or are you willing to build enough memory into your computer system so that you can use a scanner that scans to RAM only? (The scanned image can, of course, be saved to disk after the scan is complete, even in a scan-to-RAM scanning system.) And finally, of course, what does your budget allow?

Drum scanners

It's only recently that desktop scanned imagery systems have begun to approach the results achievable with the much more expensive high-end drum scanners from such firms as Scitex, Hell Graphics and Crosfield. Even now these high-end systems maintain advantages for certain uses. Although desktop systems can achieve the same resolution that service bureaus using the high-end equipment typically provide, the difference between the drum scanning mechanism of the high-end systems and the moving scan head mechanisms typically used in desktop scanners for example, is like the difference between camera lenses of differing qualities. It's possible to get a sharper, clearer picture with the better system.

Because the established drum scanning systems are expensive and require highly trained technicians to operate them, drum scanning is typically done through a service bureau. Some desktop image-editing software can import scans in the file formats produced by high-end systems. You can thus pay for a Scitex scan, for example, and then transfer it via disk to your desktop system,

Figure 1. Controlling the scan. The scanner software supplied with the Microtek MSF-300Z flatbed scanner allows cropping and adjustment of color and resolution; it also provides information on image size relative to available RAM and hard disk space.

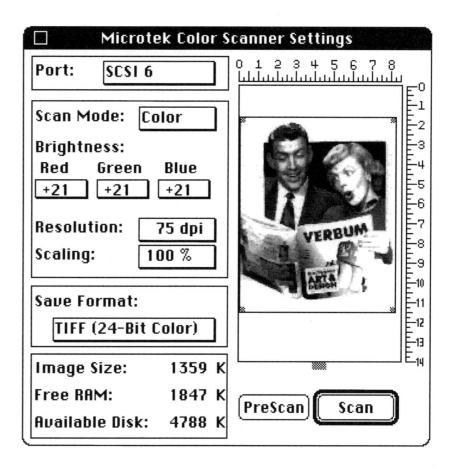

and edit it there. You'll have the high quality of a drum scan, while avoiding the expense of hiring a technician to edit the image on the high-end system. If you were to use the high-end process from start to finish, you would be facing steep costs, while being deprived of hands-on participation in the editing or retouching process.

Desktop scanners

There are five common types of scanning systems used in the desktop environment, although not all of them sit on the desktop. They are flatbed, sheetfed, overhead, hand-held, transparency and video. The type of system you use and the specific scanner you choose within that system depends on your needs. Several specific examples, which can be used with either Mac or IBM PC unless otherwise noted, are provided as each type of scanner is described in this chapter. However, scanner technology is improving rapidly, so if you're in the market for a scanning system, it's a good idea to explore before you buy — read up-to-date reviews in full-coverage computer magazines, and "test drive" several models with the types of materials you expect to scan.

Flatbed scanners

Flatbed scanners let you put a single reflective sheet face-down on the glass bed of the scanner and close the lid over it to keep out extraneous light. A scan head, driven by a motor, moves under the sheet like the imaging system in a photocopier. Flatbed scanners vary in the size of originals they will accept. They can also be used to scan pages from books (as long as the page can be flattened against the bed), thin three-dimensional items or even relatively thick ones if you can exclude (or live with) the extra light that gets in because the lid is propped open (see Figure 2 in Chapter 1).

Standard resolution for flatbed scanners has been 300 dpi, with some models able to achieve resolutions over 300 dpi by *interpolation* (adding dots between the existing dots to smooth the image) rather than by adding any more information to the scanned image. However, newer and more expensive models scan at a true 400 dpi, and interpolate to even higher resolutions.

Some flatbed scanners have adapters for scanning transparencies. But unless you have large transparencies, don't expect these adapter solutions to be even remotely equivalent to dedicated transparency scanners. Following are a few examples of flatbed scanners (by no means a comprehensive list).

The **Apple Scanner** is a grayscale scanner that scans at 1 and 4 bits, so it provides a maximum of 16 levels of gray. It accepts documents up to 8½ x 14 inches, and scanning resolution can be set at 75, 100, 150, 200 or 300 dpi. The AppleScan software bundled with the scanner allows you to adjust brightness and contrast and do grayscale editing, zooming in for a close-up view if you want to. The HyperScan software that comes with this scanner makes it ideal for scanning artwork for use in HyperCard.

If you own an Apple Scanner and want to upgrade it to full grayscale capability at 8 bits and from 72 to 300 dpi in 1 dpi intervals, you can do so with the **Abaton 8-bit Apple Upgrade** installed by a field technician. The **Abaton Scan 300/G** has essentially the same capabilities as the Apple Scanner with the upgrade kit, but it costs less than the combined cost of scanner and upgrade.

The **Microtek MSF-300GS** grayscale scanner, which scans at 1 or 8 bits, and the **MSF-300Z** grayscale/color scanner, which scans at 1, 8 or 24 bits can scan at 16 resolutions from 75 to 300 dpi (Figure 2). They can accept originals up to 8½ x 14 inches. The scanners are operated via a desk accessory on the Mac. Both Digital Darkroom and ImageStudio are bundled (included in the package) with both scanners, and the 300Z also comes with a limited version of PhotoMac. (For descriptions of these image-editing programs, see "Image-editing software" later in this chapter.) The Microtek DA allows cropping, resizing from 25 to 400 percent, adjustment of brightness and contrast and grayscale editing at a magnified view. The 300Z records color by making three passes of the scan head, recording one of the three primaries each time.

The **Sharp JX-450** is a grayscale/color scanner that accepts originals up to 11 x 17 inches and also has an attachment for scanning 35mm slides and larger transparencies. It scans in resolutions of 30 to 300 dpi at 1, 4, 8 and 24 bits and allows cropping and adjustment of brightness and contrast. Color scanning is done in one pass.

Figure 2. Flatbed scanners. The Microtek 300Z is typical of flatbed scanners, designed to scan flat reflective originals that can be placed face-down on the bed and covered with the lid. The original stays still while the light source and scan head move.

The **Sharp JX-600 Commercial Color Scanner,** designed to scan either reflective originals or transparencies, has a stationary scan head and a moving bed. It scans originals up to 11 x 17 inches at up to 600 dpi (Figure 3). It scans at 10 bits per color (or 30 bits total), which gives 16.8 million colors. ▌ *Although 24 bits provide a range of over 16.7 million color possibilities, many 24-bit scanners record color with only 6 (rather than 8) bits of accuracy per color. A 10-bit-per-color scanner is designed to get the full 24 bits of color information.*

The **Sharp JX-100** is a small, inexpensive flatbed scanner with characteristics in common with hand-held scanners (Figure 4).

The easy-to-use **HP ScanJet Plus** grayscale flatbed scanner accepts 8½ x 11-inch originals and scans at resolutions from 12 to 300 dpi in 1 dpi increments, and also at 600 dpi by interpolation from a true resolution of 300 dpi. Scans can be 1, 4 or 8 bits deep. DeskScan and DeskPaint software are supplied with the scanner. Brightness and contrast controls are provided.

The **La Cie Silverscanner** scans at 300 dpi in one pass for all three colors. It records at 300 dpi and interpolates at 50 to 600 dpi and accepts up to 8½ x 11-inch originals.

The **Agfa Focus II 800GSE** is a 400 dpi grayscale scanner with 14 steps of resolution, including interpolation at 500, 600, 700 and 800 dpi. It scans originals up to 8¼ x 12¾ inches at 1, 6 and 8 bits. McViewPlus software provides cropping, resizing to any size, brightness and contrast control and grayscale editing in enlarged views.

Sheetfed scanners

Sheetfed scanners are designed to automatically feed a stack of pages, one at a time, past a scanning mechanism. They are ideal for OCR (optical character recognition) tasks, in which the goal is to "translate" multipage documents from print on paper to electronic files. But sheet-feeding has some limitations that make these scanners inappropriate for general graphics uses: First, it's difficult or impossible to precisely control the orientation of a page going through a sheet-feeding mechanism. And second, subject matter is very restricted — to single sheets that will fit through the rollers and to sheets that are big enough not to get lost inside the machine. So you can't scan a page in a book, for example, unless you photocopy it first, and then scan the photocopy.

Figure 3. Scanning several formats. Some scanners, such as the Sharp JX-600 color scanner shown here, can scan both reflective originals and transparencies.

Figure 4. Combining scanning features. The glass window of the Sharp JX-100 scanner is placed over an original document and the light and scan head move above it, recording the image. Like hand-held scanners, this 6 x 12-inch model is very portable.

Because sheetfed scanners move the original through a mechanism, the original must be fairly sound and sturdy, and preferably square-edged. Stiff originals may bind or fail to start at all through sheet-feeders. Glossiness adds another potential source of problems — slippage and uneven feeding. Hence, a 4 x 6-inch photo may experience a number of feeding problems because of stiffness, small size and glossiness. Some sheetfed scanners are flatbeds at heart, equipped with a removable sheet-feeding mechanism. They can be converted fairly quickly to ordinary flatbed scanners.

Overhead scanners

An overhead scanner has the camera, and optionally the lights, pointing down toward a surface onto which you place the items to be scanned. This has both advantages and disadvantages: two advantages are that the original to be scanned can be thicker than a piece of paper and you can see exactly the orientation of the original. With flatbeds, you have to put the original face-down, so you can't see the precise orientation as well, and closing the flap can jar it out of alignment.

Because overhead scanning takes a bird's-eye view, there is no flap to cover the original as there is in a flatbed scanner. Being open to ambient light, overhead scanners have the disadvantage of potentially uneven or otherwise inadequate illumination. It's best to situate overhead scanners in areas where there is adequate control of the light sources, either for providing enough ambient light for a good exposure, or for keeping stray light out of self-lit systems.

The **Truvel TZ-3** is an overhead grayscale scanner (with its own fluorescent light source) that can scan originals up to 12 x 17 inches at up to 8 bits per pixel (Figure 5). Resolution can be adjusted from 75 to 900 dpi in 1 dpi increments; true resolution is 300 dpi. However, it scans to RAM only, which limits the physical size and resolution of the originals it can scan to the amount of RAM available to the scanner driver program. The TZ-3 comes with a version of the Photoshop image-editing program.

Hand-held scanners

Among the least expensive and in some ways the most versatile of the grayscale and color scanners are the hand-held models. Small and portable, they can scan "anywhere a mouse can go" — scanning a book page or the fabric on an upholstered chair, for example — as long as it's within the reach of the cord that plugs into an interface box that then plugs into a port on the computer (Figure 6). A hand-held scanner has no motor since it's moved manually, and it has its own built-in light source that illuminates an original as the scanner is rolled over the original and the scan head picks up the reflected light. Most hand-held scanners scan relatively narrow strips (2½ to 5 inches) into RAM rather than to disk.

Scanning larger originals in several passes and assembling the parts with image-editing software doesn't always give good results. Hand-held scanners

Figure 5. Overhead scanning. Overhead scanners such as this Truvel TZ-3 allow you to position documents face-up so that you can precisely control position and orientation. They also make it easy to scan three-dimensional objects.

Figure 6. Scanning by hand. A hand-held scanner records a relatively narrow strip of image as it's dragged over an original document. Some hand-held scanners have software for reassembling several side-by-side strips into a wider image.

can be surprisingly precise, even if the speed at which they're dragged varies. The best guarantee of a geometrically undistorted scan is to apply only light pressure to the scanning head, just over and behind the wide rubber roller, and to make sure to apply no side-to-side motion as you drag. Perform nonrecording test passes to ensure that you won't bump into desktop obstacles during your scanning stroke. If you move too fast for the image data to be fed to your computer, you'll lose parts of the image, and you'll have to rescan.

It's possible for other software—for example, a periodic alarm utility, electronic mail handling, networking software or background tasks — to interfere with the data flow of hand-scanning. All these will require some of your CPU's time, and could possibly disturb the data stream. Additionally, any active RAM-resident software you may have, in the form of DAs, TSRs or background tasks, take up RAM space that could be productively allotted to the scanning function. So reduce concurrent activities to a minimum when using a hand-held scanner.

Thunderware's **LightningScan** scans a 4.2-inch wide strip whose length is limited only by the amount of RAM available to hold the image. The scanner supports up to 32 shades of gray. It comes with a snap-on guide that can be used to align the scanner with a straightedge to reduce dragging errors during the scan. In addition, the bundled ThunderWorks software provides an easy, intuitive way for scanned strips to be joined to reconstruct a whole image.

The Logitech **ScanMan** scanners for Mac and PC provide scans that are 4.2 inches wide and limited in length only by the amount of RAM. They are capable of recording up to 32 shades of gray per pixel. It comes with scan-control software that has a moderate degree of image adjustment and editing capabilities.

Slide scanners

In general, slide scanners are the "desktop" method of choice for reproducing photographs for full-color reproduction in print. Although most graphic designers would agree that for the most demanding printing jobs the quality achieved by these systems doesn't equal that achieved by high-end scanners, slide scanners can produce images that work well in many publishing applications. For color image reproduction, slide scanners achieve better results than flatbed models because they are designed expressly to scan at higher resolution and high accuracy. The entire scanning apparatus and light source is self-contained and some are self-calibrating, which reduces the number of variables that can affect the quality of the scan. ∎ *For slide scanners, resolution is often expressed in terms of pixels (768 x 512 pixels, for example), rather than dots per inch, because they are designed to scan the full frame of a 35mm slide, which is a standard size and width-to-height ratio (3:2).*

Slide scanners vary in the way they handle color calibration and in how they enable you to preview the scan. Color calibration ensures that variations in the color and brightness of the light source are taken into consideration during the scan. A preview scan provides a lower-resolution on-screen version of the image so that you can correct color, and even choose an area of interest, before investing the time necessary for a full scan.

Three slide scanners for producing images for the Macintosh are the Barneyscan CIS-3515, the Nikon LS-3500 and the Howtek Scanmaster 35/II. All three can save scanned images in EPS, PICT2 and TIFF file formats.

The Barneyscan CIS-3515 scans quickly and is bundled with excellent software (BarneyscanXP, which is a dedicated version of what is now Adobe Photoshop for the Macintosh) for manipulating the image after scanning. This scanner provides a single input resolution (1024 x 1500 pixels), can produce four-color separations and saves in formats that can be used by Mac, PC, Amiga and Targa systems. The preview scan that's provided for cropping, exposure control and gamma adjustment is a 256-shade grayscale image.

The Howtek Scanmaster 35/II scans at 2048 x 3000 pixels and provides automatic focus but manual color calibration. It previews in color, allowing exposure control, gamma adjustment and sharpening of the image before the final scan. No postscan image manipulation is provided and no color separation. Files can be saved in Mac, PC and Amiga formats.

The **Nikon LS-3500** provides automatic color calibration and focus and a top scan resolution of 4096 x 6144 pixels, with seven lower settings as well (Figure 7). The color preview scan can be cropped, controlled for exposure and gamma-adjusted before the final scan is made, but no image-editing capabilities are provided, so postscan manipulation must be done outside the scanner-driver software. The software can, however, directly produce four-color separation files.

Using a light sensor different from the typical CCD, the **Array Technologies AS-1** scans in 36-bit mode and increases resolution by continuously sampling the image and averaging the results. The more samples, the better the color fidelity and resolution. The scanner operator can choose from a range of resolutions by selecting relatively short or long scanning times (longer scans provide more samples). It can scan slides, flat art or three-dimensional objects.

Still video

One of the most exciting developments in the field of digitized imaging is still video technology. Like desktop scanners, still video cameras use a solid-state "retina" or CCD array — thousands of light sensors that convert light into electrical energy. The nature of video prevents it from holding extremely sharp detail. You would not, for example, use a video image of a document page for OCR. Still video images are ideal for multimedia use in applications like SuperCard and Plus (HyperCard-like programs that also support color). For publishing purposes, their resolution is not quite acceptable, at least not with cameras at the lower end of the range.

In an electronic camera, an image is stored as analog video data on a 2-inch magnetic floppy disk. The disk holds either 25 or 50 shots, depending on the

Other digitizers

There are some digitizers that just don't fit comfortably into the flatbed, sheetfed, hand-held, overhead or transparency scanner categories. Some digitizers can read handwriting (one is called Personal Writer; another is a software-only solution called Paper Keyboard). HyperSpace can digitize in three dimensions. Some have been around for a long time, like the digitizing tablets that are common in CAD applications (Kurta, Summagraphics, CalComp and GTCO arc noted manufacturers of these). The UnMouse from MicroTouch functions like a mini, high-resolution tablet. The Mac'n Touch Screen by the same company uses the same technology right on the Macintosh screen.

MacVision from Koala can turn an inexpensive video camera into a slow framegrabbing device that sends grayscale images through the SCSI port to MacVision software. From there, the image can be saved in any number of formats. The resolution is not very high, but for basic input of three-dimensional or live subjects MacVision can be useful.

Thunderscan is a hardware-software combination that turns an Apple ImageWriter printer into a grayscale scanner that can sense 32 shades of gray at resolutions up to almost 288 dpi. The Thunderscan hardware consists of a small interface box and a reading head that temporarily replaces the printer's ribbon cartridge. The original image to be scanned is fed through the normal paper path of the printer, and the reading head scans the image. The Thunderscan software allows pixel-level retouching, as well as manipulating brightness and contrast. Paint tools such as the pencil and the eraser are available for editing images.

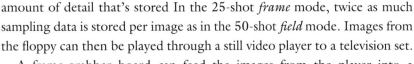

Fure 7. Scanning slides. This Nikon LS-3500 previews a slide before scanning, so that you can crop the image and adjust brightness and gamma before investing time and memory in the final scan.

Figure 8. Recording video on disk. Still video cameras record images on a floppy disk. Some cameras can also be plugged directly into a television monitor to "play" these images; others require a separate player. Still video printers can print from the floppy disk.

amount of detail that's stored In the 25-shot *frame* mode, twice as much sampling data is stored per image as in the 50-shot *field* mode. Images from the floppy can then be played through a still video player to a television set.

A frame-grabber board can feed the images from the player into a microcomputer, where they can be saved as standard-format files. A still video printer can print from the floppy. Both Canon and Sony have released color still video cameras — the Xap Shot and the Mavica — for the consumer market, in addition to much more expensive versions produced by these two companies and Nikon for high-end industrial use and for instantaneous transmission of photos (via telephone lines) for news publications such as *Time* and *USA Today.*

The **Xap Shot RC-250** can be plugged directly into a TV to act as its own player or into a digitizer to convert the image for use on the computer, although the **RV-301 player,** with remote control, provides a better image than the Xap Shot's built-in player and can also be plugged into a Canon color copier. The **Canon RP-420** color video printer provides a way to output still video images. The Xap Shot accepts alternate lenses, including a macro lens that allows for quite well-focused shots at 12 inches or closer. The **Canon RC-470** has a two-position zoom lens.

The **Sony Mavica MVC-A10** doesn't plug into a TV or digitizer directly, but instead requires an adapter box, the **MAP-T2 Adapter** (Figure 8). The Mavica accepts no extra lenses and can shoot focused, centered pictures at five feet or more. Computer Friends now has a graphics adapter board for the Mac that will interface with the Canon still video camera as well as traditional NTSC and RGB camera sources.

Video capture

Some video capture cards (see "Video" in Chapter 1) are dedicated to this purpose and are installed in the computer as additional boards, while others, such as the Truevision Targa for the PC, combine video capture features with the color graphics adapter function that also drives the monitor. This results in a cost savings and also leaves a slot free for other add-on boards. Even though a 24-bit frame-grabber board can display its images on an 8-bit graphics adapter, a 24-bit display board is required for full preview and control of color. Scion's **Media Master** incorporates 24-bit capture and display for the Macintosh. Other companies that make 24-bit display boards as well as frame grabbers include **Computer Friends, Mass Microsystems, RasterOps** and **Radius.** The relatively inexpensive **Computer Eyes** video capture boards for the Mac or PC offer 8-bit grayscale capture and 8- or 24-bit color capture. Some video capture boards, such as the **NuVista Plus,** are better adapted than others for capturing still video.

One of the best ways to capture video is via a separate encoder/decoder to a frame-grabber board that accepts RGB video. The combination Truevision system of the **VIDI/O Box** and a **Vista** card, for example, bypasses some of the image degradation that can happen with a board that captures a composite video signal directly.

One of the most affordable ways to perform video editing on the desktop is with an Amiga. With this economical but powerful platform, video output with *genlock* (the function that locks together the computer-generated and the video signals) is a standard feature, and a number of video-editing packages provide relatively sophisticated capabilities at a low price. Screen resolution is lower than on a Mac or Targa-equipped PC, but live video capture and manipulation can be performed quite readily.

LIVE!2000 is a real-time video frame grabber for the Amiga 2000, and Invision is a real-time video special-effects package. Together they allow you to view and combine two live video inputs, with fades, blends and other special effects.

The **Video Toaster** brings the Amiga up to broadcast video quality (Figure 9). It provides real-time manipulation of incoming live video, a character generator, color processing and rendering of 24-bit 3D images and paintings. Its frame grabber can capture up to eight consecutive NTSC fields at $\frac{1}{60}$ second, and it can store up to 1000 video still frames to disk.

Figure 9. Bringing video to the desktop. The Video Toaster hardware-and-software combination brings broadcast-quality video to the desktop via the Amiga platform.

Storage media

When you work with digitized images, you need large amounts of disk space, both for managing the scan itself and for storing intermediate versions of images edited with image-manipulation software. Although one of the trends in the development of image-editing software is the addition of object-oriented (even PostScript-based) drawing and layering capabilities, the images produced by image-editing programs are still only sophisticated paint files — a single layer of colored pixels spread out to form an image.

Once you make a few changes to an image, there is no easy way to restore the previous version of the picture. You need to save several versions as your image develops so you can go back — without going all the way back to the original scanned image — if you make a mistake or change your mind. The image-editing process becomes a balancing act between saving backup files and tying up large amounts of disk space. And because many image-editing programs work back and forth between RAM and hard disk as files are edited, transfer time in storing and retrieving files is also important. Hard disk drives, removable media and various optical systems provide options.

Hard disk drives

The heart of most microcomputer data storage systems is the hard disk drive that stores the operating system — in Macintosh parlance, the System file — and the application programs. To operate efficiently, you need a fairly large amount of free space available on this hard drive. The available space is usually composed of several smaller blocks of space rather than one big block, and files

File compression

Once you start working with scanned imagery, it won't be too long before large numbers of these bulky files accumulate and begin to crowd any storage medium you have. There are several ways to make your image files more manageable by reducing the amount of disk space required to store the image data. The best approach to use varies based on the type of image and its end use. The ideal situation would provide immediate access to the images via a quick compress/decompress process with no loss of quality. There are several Macintosh applications that compress all types of files — for example, StuffIt Deluxe from Aladdin Systems and Disk Doubler from Salient. A kind of compression targeted especially at full-color images is *JPEG*. JPEG offers dramatic savings in disk space, reducing, for example, a 1000K image to 100K or less with no loss of detail. More extreme compression ratios are possible, but detail is lost as the ratio increases.

The JPEG compression process is available as software from several sources. There are two Photoshop plug-ins that perform JPEG compression and decompression. Studio/32 will decompress JPEG files. A stand-alone package, called PicturePress is also available. A companion hardware product in the form of a Macintosh NuBus card reduces compression/decompression time from minutes to seconds.

Black-and-white bitmaps can be compressed to a small fraction of their size; they respond well to the general compression utilities. Eight-bit color and grayscale images compress well, but the compression ratio varies substantially and is generally less than that for 1-bit images. Savings are even less for 24-bit images. Although savings vary widely with the type of image, its intricacy and its use of color, here are some figures obtained from compressing the same image in various forms with StuffIt:

24-bit TIFF, 10 percent savings
8-bit TIFF, 17 percent savings
1-bit TIFF, 20 percent savings

The JPEG-compressed 24-bit image, retaining high quality, yielded a spectacular 93 percent savings.

Compression and decompression add time to the process of using an image in a layout, and the files are not generally accessible, as they were before, directly by graphics applications, unless the graphics programs have been upgraded to handle compressed formats.

will be split so they can fit into the smaller spaces. The more complex the job of fitting the files into the spaces and retrieving and linking the parts again when you call them up, the longer the saving and opening processes will take. Also, the disk with the operating system is the one that temporarily stores files while work is in progress. For instance, a color image-editing program can take over some of the hard disk space to store a scanned image that's too large to be retained in RAM during editing.

An efficient system for working with scanned images requires a large hard disk. Large means not only high-capacity, but also having a good percentage of free space. If you buy a new hard disk drive, it's worth the extra money to get one with the fastest access time (20 milliseconds or less), and the highest capacity you can comfortably afford. Note that the price difference between a 40 and a 60 MB drive may be less than $100. The jump from a 60 to an 80 MB drive may be less than that. Even low-volume scanning will inevitably start crowding your disk, so shop carefully, and buy with future needs in mind. Periodically, clear your drive of old files, and run an optimizing utility program occasionally — one from a utilities package such as Norton Utilities, for example — to consolidate small segments of disk space into larger, more efficiently used ones. (Another way to increase storage efficiency is to use compression software to reduce the size of files to be archived or to be stored for transfer to a service bureau for output.)

Removable media

Between the largest hard disks and the floppy that holds between 1 and 2 MB are portable hard disk cartridges that hold about 45 MB. These are convenient for transporting large files to a service bureau for output, for example, and for quick backup.

The **Bernoulli box** was the first broadly used technology for removable hard disks. Originally the cartridges held about 20 MB of data, but newer portable models accept special 45 MB cartridges. There is now also a dual-drive model, about the size of a pizza box. With these double cartridges, you can make quick backups of large files, and have 90 MB of removable on-line storage. The Bernoulli cartridges are lightweight and durable.

With the exception of the Bernoulli box, most of the removable 44 MB hard drives, are based on a **SyQuest** mechanism and cartridges. They all use Winchester disk technology that sucks the air and dust away from the disk medium. The primary differences in SyQuest drives arise in the software provided by each manufacturer to format the cartridges, and in mechanical characteristics such as fan effectiveness. The fact that any SyQuest cartridge can at least be read (if not written to) in any SyQuest drive lends them a degree of universality that adds a great deal to their convenience. However, because the cartridges are in effect hard disks in a plastic shell, they need more careful handling, and storage than Bernoulli cartridges.

Optical storage

One of the major benefits of optical storage, besides the ability to hold mountains of images, is that the data is relatively safe from factors such as magnetic fields and head crashes that can ruin magnetic media. Since nothing touches the surface of the disk, or comes dangerously close to it, optical disks are a nearly ideal storage medium.

Optical storage in the form of prerecorded compact disks (CDs) is extremely space-efficient, since a single CD can hold several hundred MB of data. CD ROM (compact disk read-only memory) is the storage medium often used for digitized stock photo collections, like those offered by NEC, Comstock and Tsunami Press (Figure 10).

Write once, read many, or *WORM,* technology is expensive, but it has a place in archival storage where final versions of images may be stored and retrieved. It's a sturdy medium with a long data life. One limitation of WORM drives is that you can't reuse the same place on the disk for new data. All new data is placed on previously unused surface, which eventually gets used up. On the other hand, with the right software, this technology allows you to locate older versions of images and other files, because their original data is undisturbed. Unless you have reason to archive your work, WORM systems are an unnecessary limitation.

Removable erasable optical memory, or *REOM,* drives behave like magnetic disks, in that they are fully "rewritable," but they're generally slower than most hard disks. An optical drive is standard on the NeXT computer. Some optical drives have a built-in RAM cache system that increases their effective speed by initially storing data temporarily in solid-state memory and writing it to disk at more opportune moments, so that the computer doesn't have to wait for the disk-writing operation to be completed. A single REOM drive costs more than a similarly capacious magnetic drive, but the optical disks are *removable* cartridges. As you store more data on more optical cartridges, your cost per MB will drop dramatically over adding more magnetic drives.

Display devices

If you can afford any kind of display system you want, consider a 19-inch 24-bit full-color monitor. The Sony Trinitron, sold under several computer monitor labels, provides good quality. However, for some fraction of the cost of the large color monitor, you can get a 21-inch grayscale monitor with full 8-bit or 4-bit grayscale, *and* a 13-inch 24-bit color monitor. Putting the grayscale monitor in front of you and the color off to the side will provide you with both a double-page spread for laying out the publications into which your digitized images go and a full-color view for detailed work on scanned images. Grayscale monitors provide a sharper image and are easier on the eyes than color screens; they also produce less ELF (extremely low-frequency) radiation, which has come to be seen as a health concern.

Figure 10. Using photographic clip art. This image is a combination of two photos from Tsunami Press's The Right Image collection of clip art. Several stock photo services make their images available on CD ROM disks or by tele-communication via modem.

Another compromise for the sake of keeping costs down is to get a color monitor with an 8-bit video card. In this case it's a good idea to choose a card that can be upgraded later to 24-bit. For any monitor, consider the amount of radiation emitted and the scan rate, which is expressed in megahertz (MHz). The higher the rating, the more stable the image on-screen. Below 60 MHz a definite flicker can be seen on-screen, especially when the monitor is situated where natural light falls, so there are few monitors below 60 MHz. Many are 60-70 MHz; those at 70-80 MHz provide a better picture but they also tend to emit more radiation.

Another factor to consider in choosing a monitor is the on-screen resolution (dots per inch displayed on screen). On the Macintosh platform, for example, the original standard was 72 dpi, which provides a 1:1 ratio between the size you see on the screen and the size that's printed out. Screens with resolutions as high as 82 or 85 dpi provide a sharper image, but they also display images at a smaller size than they will print. You lose the direct 1:1 ratio at these higher resolutions, but you can also see more of an image or a page without having to switch to a reduced view.

On DOS-based machines, choose a VGA-or-better display system, with enough color depth to provide you with a good, true-color look at your scans. Good-quality large-screen display systems are not inexpensive, but they're an excellent investment.

On the IBM PC-compatible platform the Targa standard is almost as important for display as it is for video capture. Five Targa models support 8, 16, 24 and 32 bits per pixel, as well as real-time capture and genlock abilities for video interfacing. Hercules also makes a (less expensive) color graphics board that's set up for video input and output.

Another consideration in choosing a 24-bit monitor is color calibration. One of the most difficult aspects of working with digitized color images is getting the color of the printed image to match what you see on-screen. A color calibration device for the monitor can help with this by ensuring that monitor color stays consistent. The Radius PrecisionColor Calibrator, for example, is a device that will calibrate Radius color and grayscale displays or an Apple 8-bit color/grayscale system. It uses an optical sensor that attaches to the screen and adjusts voltage to the monitor according to various specifications, such as true Pantone colors, ambient lighting or gamma preferences for scanned and captured video images. The Calibrator from Barco is a microprocessor-controlled monitor and optical sensor that requires an additional display card and that provides full digital control.

Regardless of what monitor(s) you buy, look also at the possibility of increasing the speed of your display system. Graphics accelerator boards can significantly cut the time you spend waiting for the screen to redraw when you make a change to an image. The degree of acceleration depends on your software. Typically, the screen-refresh time of painting software will be accelerated, but that of a color image editor will not be. This is because image-editing software needs to compute the appearance of each pixel based on a combination of factors including viewing mode, color depth, masks, transparencies, and stored versus displayed resolution, and thus typically requires more time to compute than to display. The best overall cure for accelerating photo-editing work is a faster CPU, which accelerates everything.

Another feature that can cut the amount of time you spend waiting for screen refresh is *hardware panning,* the use of the video card's RAM or the computer's own RAM for quickly panning to off-screen sections of a document. In this case, scrolling the scene is controlled by a fast, single-purpose processor independent from the CPU. Typically, the available virtual screen space needed for hardware panning is obtained by trading away something else — for example, the number of colors that can be displayed.

Image-editing software

The simplest bitmaps (1-bit black-and-white images) can be edited and modified with bitmapped painting programs such as Studio/1, MacPaint II, SuperPaint 2, Canvas 2, GraphicWorks and MacCalligraphy on the Mac, and

Figure 11. Changing shades of gray. To modify this image, individual shades of gray were selected and replaced with other shades.

Dr. Halo, Windows Paint and GEM Paint on the PC. Since most scanned images are done in grayscale or in color, these black-and-white bitmap programs are not discussed here. (For specifics about using paint programs, see *The Verbum Book of Digital Painting*.) Grayscale image-editing programs are relatively less expensive than color image editors, which can work with both grayscale and color files.

Grayscale editors

Grayscale image-editing software allows you to import a grayscale file such as a scanned image, alter it by adjusting contrast, brightness and gamma, transform individual grays into other grays, paint and draw on the image using artists' tools selected from the tool palette and apply special effects. Images can be combined by cutting and pasting, or by assigning levels of transparency to some elements, so that when they are pasted in, the image underneath shows through to a greater or lesser degree.

By increasing the number of grays in a light or dark area, a grayscale editor can bring out the detail and subtle shading in that area. In effect, when you adjust gamma, you assign a different number of grays to a range on the scale of grays. The ability to alter individual shades of gray can be applied to achieve special effects within a photo image (Figure 11) or to make it possible to select certain areas of an image. For example, if the white background of an image is mottled, the light grays within it can be eliminated by manipulating them to white.

The paint tools supplied in a grayscale editor typically include the pencil, paintbrush, paint bucket and airbrush found in bitmapped painting programs (Figure 12). There are also familiar selection tools — the marquee (rectangular selection tool) and lasso (irregular shape selection tool) — for selecting

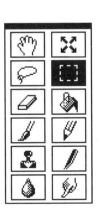

Figure 12. A grayscale tool palette. This tool palette from ImageStudio has the familiar navigation, selection and painting tools of a paint program as well as three tools for blending, smudging and smearing (the water drop, finger and charcoal) and one (the rubber stamp) for picking up part of an image and reproducing it in another place.

areas to be darkened, lightened, blurred or sharpened (Figure 13). In addition to painting and selecting by area, most programs have tools that can paint on or select by designated shades of gray. Special tools for blending, smudging and smearing help hide the "seams" in image collages. And tools that can pick up texture can be used to apply the same pattern elsewhere, functioning as "rubber stamps" (Figure 14). To select or edit part of an image, you can zoom in on it for a close-up (Figure 15).

Most 8-bit color paint programs can perform powerful grayscale image editing. They are generally easy to use and packed with special effects. Their limitation to 256 colors, however, seriously restricts their domain to less critical color work. But to edit a grayscale image, 256 *grays* are more than enough to produce high-quality grayscale works.

Figure 13. Using special effects. The right side of this photographic image was modified in Photoshop by applying effects such as Equalize, Sharpen and masking (to put in a graduated background fill).

Figure 14. Rubber stamping. Photoshop's rubber stamp tool was used to pick up and apply the texture inside the smaller square and also to contribute to the deckle edge of the border.

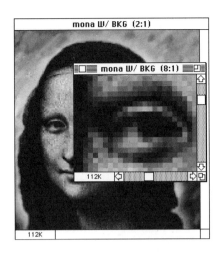

Figure 15. Zooming in. Magnified views allow image editing pixel-by-pixel.

Figure 16. Using the copy brush. Digital Darkroom's paint-brush tool was used in Copy mode to copy the locks of hair from one side of the girl's face (below left) and duplicate them on the other side (below right).

Digital Darkroom can apply all the basic grayscale photo-editing effects, such as softening and sharpening, and also offers powerful editing tools that, for example, let you select an area, apply perspective distortion to it, wrap it around a cube, render the whole cube semi-transparent, feather its edges, and then paste it, with full control over which shades of gray are pasted and how they affect the area that receives the pasted selection.

The program accepts plug-in modules, which extend its capabilities by automatically installing additional menu items, editing tools, scanner drivers and special-effects filters. Several files can be opened simultaneously, which is an advantage for comparing or combining images. Also, the copy brush lets you transfer part of one image to another by stroking it on with the brush, in Copy mode. You first select a starting point by clicking on the image to be copied. Then you start painting normally with the brush, but instead of painting in one tone, the brush paints parts of the image in which you first clicked. The copy brush works within the same document, as well as between open documents. Effectively, it combines selection, copying, pasting and feathering into one operation (Figure 16).

Selecting an area in a grayscale image can sometimes be tricky work, because of the intricacy of the path you would need to trace. Digital Darkroom has traditional selection tools but can refine the shape of the selections. Moreover, the magic wand tool offers a way to automatically select

a continuous area of similar grays. With practice, you can save hours of image editing with this tool.

Digital Darkroom has the unusual capability of colorizing selected areas of a grayscale image. This is different than brushing on color. By selecting an area with any combination of selection tools, the user specifies the shade of a transparent overlay of any color. Many overlays can be used on a single document. Each one remains an independent object that can be recolored at any time, enabling you to experiment by quickly applying different colors to the overlays. Uses for quick colorizing might include changing the color of a car exterior, the fabric on a sofa or an item of clothing or the exteriors of buildings. The colorized image can be exported as a 24-bit color bitmap.

Enhance is a technical image-manipulation program that works in both 8-bit grayscale and 8-bit color. It provides a nearly CAD-like approach to the manipulation and analysis of grayscale images. It has specialized tools for determining the center of mass of an area, or for measuring its perimeter. In addition to a ruler for linear measurements, another tool provides angular measurement. The program can scale by converting pixel measurements to real-world units (3 pixels per centimeter, for example). It can open files in TIFF, PICT, EPSF and Text.

Enhance has a large selection of filters, many of which are designed not strictly for optical effects, but for bringing out hidden information from the image. You can also create your own filter effects. The program can store versions of an image in a set of three *buffers* that can be viewed in thumbnail form and called up at any time for side-by-side comparison, cutting and pasting, and further manipulation. Its toolbox offers typical painting tools, an all-important smudging tool for edge work, and flexible navigation and magnification tools. Unlike most photo-editing applications, Enhance also offers tools that create geometric shapes. You can create a 1-bit protective mask by painting it on as a black overlay or by selecting areas and filling them with black.

Gray F/X from Xerox Imaging Systems is a dedicated grayscale editing program that gives PC users capabilities like those of Digital Darkroom on the Mac. It provides full graymap control, but PC users will need to soup up their machines with extended memory to take full advantage of this program.

ImagEdit, bundled with IBM's Pagescanner for the PC, provides 8-bit grayscale editing under Microsoft Windows, though only 64 gray levels can be seen on-screen at a time. It drives a number of other scanners including those from Dest, Microtek, Canon and Hewlett-Packard, and provides grayscale editing and output in EPSF, TIFF or any IBM publishing system format.

Image-In provides modules for painting, OCR, raster-to-vector conversion, scanning and grayscale editing. The last module, called Image-In Plus, provides basic grayscale control for making global or selective changes in brightness and contrast, sharpening and blurring, and so on.

ImageStudio's easy-to-understand tool set and menu selections offer good control over the overall image and its details. The program provides all the standard photo-editing tools, including an edge-softening water drop and edge-smudging finger (see Figure 12). A charcoal predictably darkens stroked areas. ImageStudio can convert black-and-white halftoned scans to grayscale images, provided you specify the size of the halftone cell used in dithering the original. ImageStudio opens only one image file at any one time, but it can handily open several windows on a given file. In one window you can zoom in on details, while another can provide an overall view (Figure 17). Other uses for multiple views include general browsing, long-distance cutting and pasting, and referencing one part of an image while editing another.

ImageStudio can easily perform most of the frequently used photo-editing tasks, and can also apply special effects such as posterizing or embossing an image. Its selection tools are the marquee and the lasso, but these have no special abilities other than those offered by a typical painting application.

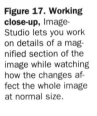

Figure 17. Working close-up, Image-Studio lets you work on details of a magnified section of the image while watching how the changes affect the whole image at normal size.

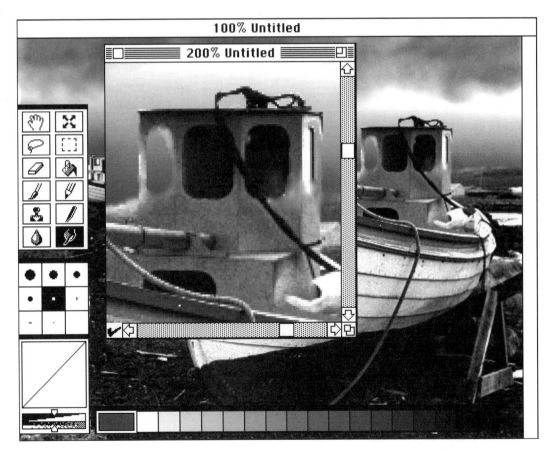

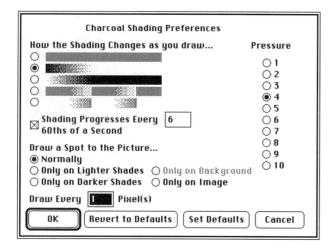

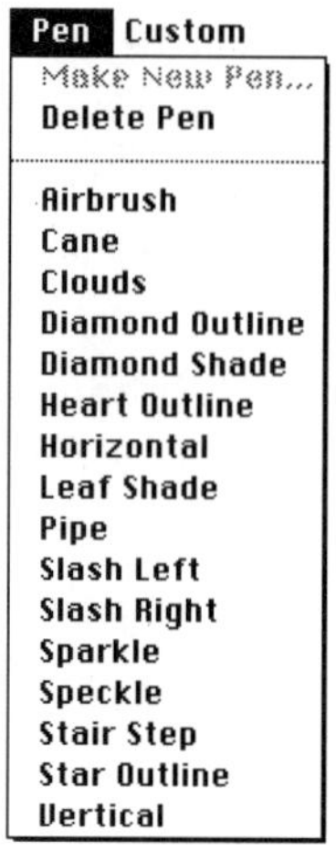

Figure 18. Customizing tools. Image-Studio's tools can be customized (either temporarily or with new default settings) through dialog boxes that control how the tools operate. Shown here are settings for the charcoal tool.

Figure 19. Adding new tools. In Image-Studio, besides customizing tools in the standard palette, you can name custom tools and make them available as menu choices.

Selected items can be moved and resized, and the brightness and contrast within a selection can be manipulated apart from the main document.

ImageStudio's tool set can be customized with settings that, for example, instruct a brush to run out of paint as the stroke proceeds (Figure 18), or by capturing a pattern from the image and saving it as a modified stamping tool. You can name your custom tools and reuse them at any time on any document (Figure 19). A separate set of modules, ImageStudio Effects, can be purchased and installed to provide free rotation, and drop shadows.

PC Paintbrush IV Plus provides a palette of up to 256 colors, and its interface is very straightforward. Though its roots are in painting, it incorporates useful retouching features. For less than $200, this program provides color/grayscale editing for the masses.

Picture Publisher is available for both PC, and Macintosh. Some of its key features include calibration from input to output device — for your own configuration or your service bureau, a feature conspicuously lacking in most grayscale programs. It also provides convenient settings of highlight, midtone and shadow values. It can manage nine clipboard areas at once and can use a hard disk as virtual memory. Antialiasing, or smoothing of jagged edges, is automatic.

It features flexible masking for montaging images or for protecting part of an image from change. It lets you create custom filters for applying special effects to image areas. Picture Publisher has an optimized form of printing halftones on laser printers called ScatterPrint. This is a form of halftoning that uses varying diffusions of fine dots to produce the levels of gray. It has integrated Super VGA support and direct EMS (extended memory support), and includes drivers for directly controlling scanners and frame grabbers for digitizing within the program.

Color image editors

Color image editors add color to grayscale tools and capabilities. Sophisticated painting programs are acquiring the powers of photo-editing applications, and photo-editing applications are acquiring tools for originating images. Color photo-retouching must deal with a complex set of variables — not a mere 256 tones, but thousands of colors. It's a data-intensive world in which 1 square inch of high-resolution image takes up about 260 K of disk space, and several times that much to manipulate it in RAM. Generally speaking, any 24-bit color paint program can be used to do a substantial amount of high-quality editing. The working difference is in the way each type of program applies a given effect.

Photo editors excel at some image-editing chores that are the counterparts of conventional photographic and retouching techniques such as darkening and lightening, altering the color balance and selective re-colorizing. Beyond conventional techniques, they also make it relatively easy to select, manipulate, and combine sections. They all offer tools designed specifically for working on the edges of pasted objects to make them appear to fit into some new scene, helping a montage look more coherent. As with grayscale image editors, there are tools for sharpening or softening and for adjusting brightness and contrast. Many photo-editors also offer gamma adjustment, which lets the user precisely alter the response curve for each of the primary colors.

The selection tools of full-color image editors generally include a rectangle, and free-form (lasso) selector, as well as an auto-selection tool, which is the equivalent of Digital Darkroom's magic wand, but with a different set of controls for working in a multimillion-color environment. Some applications let you set the sensitivity of the auto-selector so that its search for similar colors can accept only very similar colors or slightly similar colors. The method of auto-selection and its controls and options vary with each application.

Most color image editors can offer a way to protect, or *mask,* parts of the image from editing. The mask can be the shape of a selection or can be built up of multiple selections. The mask serves as a protective coat against applied paint or effects. With full-color 24-bit editors, the mask is like an 8-bit grayscale image that can be edited with painting tools. With an 8-bit mask, pure black and pure white can be designated to either protect completely or not protect at all, and shades of gray protect according to their intensity. This type of variable protection is a powerful tool for achieving or enhancing realism or for producing special effects.

With many color image editors, you can work with large images that would more than fill the RAM available on the computer. Instead of keeping an open image document RAM-resident, these programs use hard disk space to hold the excess that can't fit in RAM. With sufficient room on your hard disk, this scheme makes it possible to have several files open so that you can cut and paste among them. With large, or multiple, open files, the speed of your hard drive becomes a significant factor in the response-time needed for your operations. You'll feel a lag more if you use an older hard drive or an uncached optical drive, both which are typically slower than the recent generation of hard disks.

Although when you edit full color images it would be ideal to work with a full (24-bit or better) color display, full-color applications let you use a 256-color display system. This 8-bit display can't simultaneously show all the colors of a photographic image, but it adapts to that limitation by rendering the image with the best possible 256 colors out of 16.7 million. Color image-editing programs offer the capability to convert a full-color image to a dithered image that has fewer colors and requires far less storage space. A well-dithered 8-bit version of a 24-bit image can look quite lifelike.

ColorStudio is a 24-bit photo-editing program that provides exceptional overall color management and output on a high-end prepress system. It incorporates the same basic interface philosophy and working philosophy as ImageStudio. The program can be expanded by adding scanner and printer drivers and custom tools. You can obtain add-ons as they're available from Letraset or third parties, and install them using a utility supplied with the program.

Each image in ColorStudio has two implicit layers, an RGB layer, for the image itself, and an 8-bit mask layer, which can be viewed and manipulated independently or together with the RGB layer. When images are combined each RGB layer can interact with its own mask, and you can preview the results of pasting before locking the pasted object in place. When you copy an area of the image, you also copy its portion of the mask layer. When you paste that selection, its mask and the mask of the receiving area can interact in a variety of ways, enabling effects such as placing an image only inside the borders of typed text, applying a variable transparency across the pasted area or ignoring the white parts of the pasted section. ColorStudio's auto-selector accepts a variety of different criteria for automatically grabbing contiguous image areas. For example, you can specify the range of colors to seek. Edge feathering is available for selected objects, and you can choose whether the feathering expands outward or inward from the selection's edges.

The mask is a key ingredient in many of ColorStudio's effects. If you want to change the colors of a rose without affecting its texture you can select it, and copy its values (brightness ranges) to the mask layer; then, using the brush in Colorize mode, you can simply brush on new colors. The darks and lights of the image are protected by the mask, and only the colors change. It takes time to learn to use the mask layer, simply because it's so versatile. But ColorStudio relies on it heavily — even for some operations for which Photoshop or PhotoMac don't require a mask.

ColorStudio's tool set includes a brush, pencil, bucket, airbrush, smudging finger and water-drop. It employs floating palettes to customize the way each tool operates, to select and correct colors and determine tool shapes (Figure

20). Because its palettes can remain on-screen while you work, you can customize tools on-the-fly. Most palettes are so large, however, that on a 13-inch Apple monitor, much of your working image can become obscured. To work efficiently with ColorStudio, a large screen display is best.

ColorStudio offers a large collection of pens and brushes, each with different shapes, sizes and properties. Custom tools can be created by combining the available tool types, options and shapes and then naming and saving them to a floating palette. Custom pens can serve as your personal tool kit. Based on how you customize them, editing tools can apply color or modify it, sharpen, blur or paint with a texture you pick up from the image itself.

A frequently encountered photo-editing task is to change one color to another, or replace one range of hue, saturation and brightness values with a different combination of these three components. ColorStudio's Color Change palette lets you do all that in short order, using a double set of sliders. One set determines the affected colors, and the other set specifies the new ones.

A new annex, or add-on, called Shapes can create and import object-oriented EPS (vector) graphics, and text, which can be edited in a separate document layer that keeps it from being inextricably combined with the pixels of the image (Figure 21). With its Bezier-curve capabilities and editable text, Shapes adds a new dimension of creative possibilities to ColorStudio's repertoire. The objects in the separate layer can then be converted to expertly antialiased bitmapped images at the resolution of the document.

Figure 20. Choosing tool characteristics in ColorStudio. ColorStudio's floating palettes allow you to change the operation of such tools as the paint bucket and lasso, as well as of the paint itself.

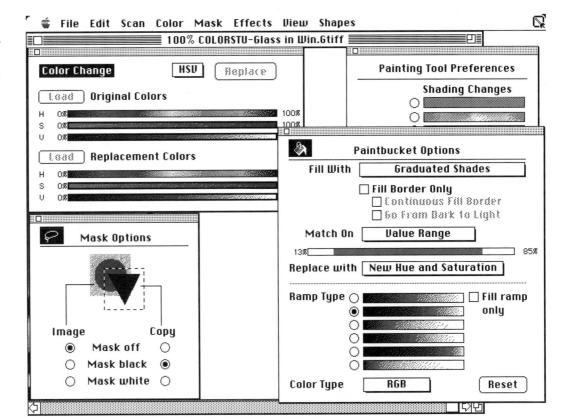

ColorStudio imports several file formats, including TIFF, PICT, PICT2 (8 to 32 bits), RIFF, Targa and Scitex. Additional translators can be added with a utility supplied with the program. RIFF files can be opened from, and saved to multiple disks. The program uses hard disk space for virtual memory. ColorStudio can serve all or most color image editing needs, from artistic to technical.

DeluxePaint (Amiga and IBM) is a tool primarily for creating art and animation, with a secondary focus on the manipulation of imported images. Still, it can be an effective program for image manipulation on the Amiga, IBM PC or the Apple II GS. While several versions of the software are available, DeluxePaint II Enhanced is probably the best suited for dealing with scanned images.

A Brush Capture feature lets the artist capture any section or element of an image and use it as a brush, so that, for example, a face could be extracted from one image and "stamped down" on a different background to create a composite image. By using the captured "brush" to paint over the projected path of an animated element, it's possible to animate the selected screen element over an unchanging but repeating background. Various brush modes such as smear, tint and blend can be used to integrate and enhance the newly created image. DeluxePaint features a Stencil function that works like a mask

Figure 21. Using the Shapes annex. Using ColorStudio with its add-on Shapes application, Jim Sweeney created each of the elements in this image separately, including the Post-Script type, and composited them with the pillar, done in StrataVision.

to lock selected areas from painting or color changes, or from animation functions.

For helping creative ideas take shape, an effect called Scanimation lets the artist digitize a sequence of scanned images such as photographs or sketches to create animation. This 8-bit program offers no color separation capabilities, but a Transparency feature lets the artist change the color of an entire background or foreground at any time by covering it with a transparent layer of color.

Images can be altered around the x, y or z axis for a "two-and-a-half dimensional" perspective in a Perspective mode that has antialiasing; this feature can be applied to animation by presetting the perspective before animating an object. Brushes can be made to operate around the x, y or z axis.

The Amiga version of DeluxePaint works in IFF format, and saves images in ILBM so that a variety of graphics programs can share the data. The IFF format is carried over to the PC version so file formats are compatible, but the PC version also supports TIFF and PCX formats.

DeluxePaint III also includes these features:

- Compatibility with all picture resolution modes lets the artist work in 320 x 200, 320 x 400, 640 x 200 or 640 x 400 pixels.
- Sixteen levels of magnification are available.
- Screen dumps can be printed with any printer the Amiga or the IBM supports, including color printers.
- Color Cycling simulates animation by repeatedly moving an object's colored pixels through a preselected range of five colors; for example, Color Cycling can make a river appear to flow.

DeskPaint 3 is a Macintosh desk accessory (DA) with a long list of image-editing talents (Figure 22). It can work with images from black-and-white to 16.7 million colors at a variety of resolutions. It opens and saves in MacPaint, PICT and TIFF formats, which makes it very useful for file-format manipulation alone. When editing full-color images on an 8-bit display, DeskPaint produces a best-fit version of the image for display. Its color dithering is generally coarser than that offered by Photoshop and Studio/32, for example. Every document window has its own set of menus, rather than the single menu typical of most DAs. DeskPaint 3 can work with several documents open at once, and it includes a folder-browsing feature that lets you step through the image files in any given folder, viewing them like a slide show, without opening and closing files.

For photo-editing, DeskPaint 3 provides paint transparency control from 0 to 100 percent for both selections and brushed-on paint. Its airbrush tool is smooth-edged and accumulates paint when it lingers over an area. A charcoal tool works somewhat like the airbrush, but additional paint is applied only while the tool is in motion. A smudging tool and color-pick-up tool nicely round out the set.

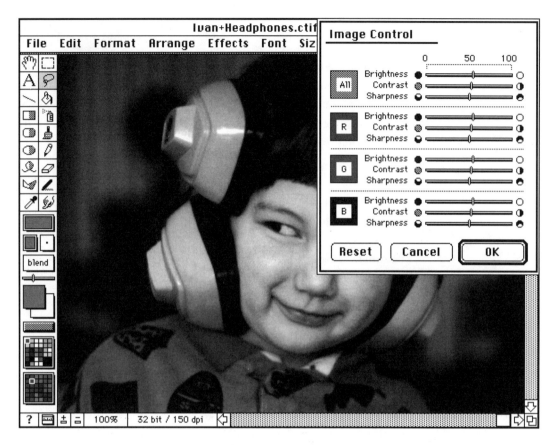

Figure 22. Using Image Control. Desk-Paint's Image Control function lets you adjust brightness, contrast and sharpness overall or for red, green or blue individually.

Figure 23. Editing a selection. Once an area of an image is selected with Desk-Paint's selection rectangle, editing options can be chosen from a palette of postselection tools.

Its selection tools include the lasso and rectangle, with the capability for the lasso to select from the inside of a selection outward, simplifying some tedious jobs. Once a selection is made, you can resize it manually or numerically, rotate it, skew it, distort it or add perspective effects. You can also produce a negative of the selected area or flip it horizontally or vertically (Figure 23). Special filters can smooth, trace edges and even apply oil-painting effects.

DeskPaint 3 supports direct text entry into text blocks that float and can be freely resized and edited until you decide to freeze the text. When a file is printed, DeskPaint 3 automatically centers a small image on a larger printing page; it also provides a print preview on request. At any time you can change the bit-depth, or maximum number of colors, of an image, going, for example, from 16.7 million colors to 256. When reducing color-depth, DeskPaint does an admirable job of dithering the available colors to fit the originals.

Digi-Paint 3 works in the Amiga's Hold-and-Modify (HAM) mode, making all 4096 colors of the Amiga palette available at once. Because it's written in assembly language, Digi-Paint 3 is an extremely fast HAM graphics program — as much as 6 to 10 times faster than other HAM programs.

The Transfer 24 software included with Digi-Paint 3 is the key to the program's image-manipulation capabilities. It lets you convert HAM pictures to any Amiga resolution and display mode (including Halfbrite and Hi-Res) with the same advanced pixel syntheses and averaging algorithms used with the Digi-View Gold video digitizer. Transfer 24 also gives you complete control of the RGB levels, contrast, brightness, saturation and sharpness of your images, as well as the ability to remap them to any palette.

The program offers 11 different drawing modes for applying paint to the screen, and Range Painting mode lets you blend colors to create smooth gradient-filled backgrounds. Colorize mode converts a black-and-white picture into lifelike color. Custom brushes can be resized, and Smoothing is Digi-Paint 3's antialiasing function for adding intermediate colors to reduce jaggies. Texture Mapping mode adds another dimension to retouching by providing several levels of warping and control over the location and type of warping (horizontal, vertical or point). Fully variable transparency produces subtle and realistic images, and it's possible to vary the amount of warping or transparency as the brush is redrawn. The program's Transparency controls add translucency to any painting operation in any drawing mode, including Texture Mapping.

Super BitMaps with Auto Scrolling allows real-time scrolling on images as large as 1024 x 1024 pixels, and navigating on a bitmap that size is easily accomplished. Digi-Paint saves and loads IFF file formats and supports all printers on the Amiga preferences list. It's designed primarily as a video — rather than print — system, however; it provides for direct video output.

Lumena is a 24-bit program for PC-compatibles that can deal with images from a variety of sources, including scanned illustrations or photos, 3D objects, video and film. It's compatible with many of the flatbed and slide scanners in use today, and can import scanned images at high resolution. You can also work live with a video camera, or grab images from videotape or videodisc.

Once the image is on-screen and ready for manipulation, the program's variable brush and pen sizes (up to 64 pixels) can create a wide variety of lines, textures and effects. Brush size and color range are pressure-sensitive, with user-definable settings for brush wetness, dry-out rate, smooth or stippled edge, color gradation direction, color source and brush shape. You can create visual libraries of unique custom brushes for quick reference, and mimic traditional media such as watercolors, gouache, pastels, oils or oriental sumi-e.

Lumena provides tools for drawing all the standard hollow and filled geometric bitmapped shapes, including antialiased shapes, as well as vector- (or object-) oriented shapes with features for standard vector graphics manipulation. For processing broad areas, the program offers effects such as brightening, color filtering, defocusing and embossing and the capability to create monochrome, mosaic or posterized effects. Transformation features range from cut, copy and paste to spin, trim and warp. Lumena's Draw mode lets you alter the qualities of the colors under the brush pad or in a defined area without affecting the image content, or expand the power of drawing tools and vector text or shapes. A Move mode works with image brushes, cells, buffers, text and vector shadows and transformation tools to alter the qualities of the image colors.

Most of the program's tools can create masks. Multilevel masking functions allow for multiple transparency levels within a mask, and can accurately separate images or backgrounds for fine tuning or color alteration. With the use of Buffers, the artist can store one or several complete images, and then pull elements from it (or the entire image) onto a new image or background. This new composite can then be manipulated with various retouch and combine features, with an "undo" command available as an ultimate safeguard. By combining the program's 250 tools with its masking capabilities, artists can create a nearly limitless range of effects.

Lumena can output to many popular color thermal, inkjet or dye sublimation printers, and to videotape and high-resolution slides. TGA is its native file format, but the program can save to BPX, EPS, color TIFF or PIX formats, and can load other nonstandard files if the header size, width and height of pixels, and number of color bits per pixel are known.

PhotoMac provides two paint tools — a bristle brush with a choice of shapes and an airbrush of variable pattern size, density and flow. You can paint with any color copied from the image itself or created with a color selector. The applied paint, or a selected area, can be made transparent to any degree from 1 to 100 percent. Partial transparency blends the underlying colors with the paint color, and repeatedly stroking the same area will build up the color. A selected area can be filled with the current choice of paint color at a preferred degree of transparency.

PhotoMac has no smudging tool for adjusting edges, nor a waterdrop tool for stroked-on softening. Edge blending is accomplished by selecting an area and instructing the program to blend the edges of the selection. This is the equivalent of feathering. You can smooth or sharpen the contents of a selected area. You can even apply a change to only the boundary pixels of a selected area.

PhotoMac can import PICT (in 8-bit format), and both TIFF and PICT2 files in 8- and 24-bit format, at any resolution. TIFF is a widely used standard for scanned images. PICT2 files are created by color paint programs, photo-retouching programs and color and grayscale scanner systems. PhotoMac can even accept a scanned color negative, and produce a positive working image. It features some convenient tools for color editing in a straightforward interface. If your Mac is equipped with Data Translation's ColorCapture board, you can input live video and capture a frame from within PhotoMac. The frame can be edited and saved like any other file. PhotoMac can also open Truevision TARGA, or VISTA images from IBM compatible platforms. The maximum size of an imported image is 32,000 x 32,000 pixels.

When working with an 8-bit display, PhotoMac offers dynamic updating of the displayed image as changes are made to the 24-bit file. When a specified

```
✓Photoshop
 Amiga IFF/ILBM
 CompuServe GIF
 EPS
 MacPaint
 PICT File
 PICT Resource
 PIXAR
 PixelPaint
 Raw
 Scitex CT
 TGA
 ThunderScan
 TIFF
```

Figure 24. Facilitating file transfer. Besides opening files for editing, Photoshop can act as a file-transformation program to pass files between programs that don't accept one another's formats.

```
 Add Noise...
 Blur
 Blur More
 Custom...
 Despeckle
 Diffuse...
 Edge Detection
 Facet
 Find Edges
 Fragment
 Gaussian Blur...
 High Pass...
 Maximum...
 Median...
 Minimum...
 Mosaic...
 Motion Blur...
 Offset...
 Pinch...
 Ripple...
 Sharpen
 Sharpen Edges
 Sharpen More
 Sphereize
 Trace Contour...
 Twirl...
 Unsharp Mask...
 Wave...
 Zigzag...
```

Figure 25. Applying effects with filters. One use of Photoshop's alpha channels is to apply special effects, called *filters*, to some areas of an image while protecting other areas. Shown here are the filters supplied with the program.

amount of idle time passes, PhotoMac automatically recomputes the best 256 display colors and refreshes the screen. Fairly sophisticated color separation settings are also available, but Adobe's recommended frequencies and angles are not yet supported. The program supports DCS format for placing preseparated color images into QuarkXPress.

Photoshop's intuitive approach to image editing presents a powerful set of features in a streamlined and elegant interface. The combined power of its tools, modes, options and special layers is not immediately apparent, so even though productive work can be done with little hands-on time, there's enough there to keep a professional experimenting for quite awhile. Photoshop can be expanded with easily added image-transformation filters and scanner-drivers. It can import and export more than a dozen file formats including EPS, TIFF, PICT file, PICT resource, Amiga IFF/ILBM, Compuserve GIF, MacPaint, PIXAR, PixelPaint, Scitex CT, TGA and Thunderscan (Figure 24). Given enough information, it can even import files in new or undocumented formats.

A selection made with any tool can be expanded, with a keystroke, to include areas of similar colors — even noncontiguous areas of similar colors everywhere in the image. Using selection tools and key modifiers, you can add or subtract areas from an existing selection. For improved editing, you can even toggle the selection's shimmering edges on and off. You can also quickly toggle between selected and unselected areas. Selection tools offer a quick way to mask the rest of the document from accidental change. Editing actions affect only the selected areas.

Instead of one mask per file, Photoshop allows any single file to have multiple layers, or *channels*. In a typical Photoshop RGB file there would be a channel for the composite image plus one channel each for red, green, and blue. There are several additional multipurpose channels called *alpha channels*. Each alpha channel can hold an 8-bit grayscale mask. The mask can be formed from one or more selected areas of any shape. You can edit the combined image channel, which affects all component colors simultaneously, or you can edit each color channel separately. Each channel is maintained in register with the original image, and each can be used to perform various masking operations and other effects on the image. Saving the precise shape of a selected area in an alpha channel enables you to reselect that area at any time, by calling up the appropriate alpha. Multiple alpha channels enable you to save several selection shapes in one document, sparing you from painstakingly reselecting the same area by hand several times. Extensive options exist for specifying the ways that different channels and files can interact with each other and with the image channels (Figure 25).

Photoshop's editing tools extend the typical set found in retouching software (Figure 26). The eraser, pencil, brush, airbrush, smudger and edge-softening water drop are there, plus a sharpening tool, a graduated-fill tool for linear or radial gradients, an antialiased (nonjaggy) line with optional arrow-heads and a rubber stamp that lets you easily duplicate part or all of an image simply by painting it on, instead of copying and pasting. Both the eraser and the rubber stamp tool can erase a part of the current image down to its last saved version—a significant time-saver when it's too late for Undo and Revert would force you to lose other changes that you want to keep. Most tools have customization settings for how quickly they act and what aspects of the image they change. Some basic modes include Normal, Color Only, Darken Only, and Lighten Only. The paintbrush and airbrush can respond to pressure-sensing digitizing tablets, such as those made by Wacom.

You can vary the transparency of the paint applied by the brush, airbrush, rubber stamp and pencil from 0 to 100 percent. Custom tool shapes (64 x 64 pixels) and custom color patterns can be made from any rectangular image chunk. Paste Controls let you modify the interaction of a pasted selection and the receiving area, so you can separately control the overall transparency and the high and low ranges of each color in the final overlay. For example, you could prevent all blues in the selection from being pasted or protect the bright yellows of the background from being affected.

Photoshop's color separation is sophisticated, allowing you to limit the amount of ink build-up or total color and to specify transfer percentages for the four colors in five steps, to compensate for dot gain on the press. It also supports Adobe's recommended screen frequencies and angles, and it uses a separation algorithm that, according to its creators, outperforms those in other programs. The pre-separated EPS file can be imported into page layout programs like QuarkXPress (Figure 27). Prepress people are often delighted by the Transfer Functions dialog box. A special set of adjustments helps you calibrate monitor colors to printed colors. Overall, Photoshop makes power-ful photo-editing accessible and painless.

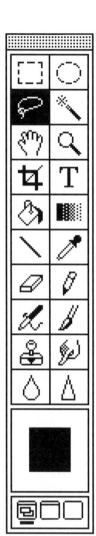

Figure 26. Photo-shop's tools. Photoshop's tools include the standard set found in most image-editing programs. Tools can be used in any of several modes, and their effects can be customized.

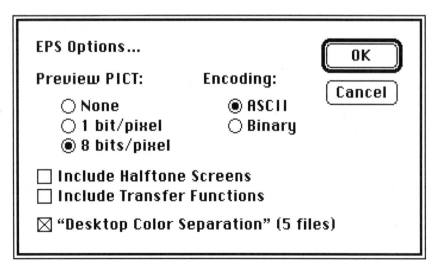

Figure 27. Saving in EPS format. The "Desktop Color Separation" (or DCS) format is useful for placing Photoshop images in page layout programs, such as QuarkXPress. The five files that make up this format include the four color separations (CMYK) and a color PICT for on-screen viewing.

PixelPaint 2 The PixelPaint tools and effects that apply to photo-editing include a spray can, or airbrush, which sprays a pattern of variable size and density. The pattern's size can be numerically specified and the degree of coverage is time-based — if left in place the airbrush will add more and more color. Spatter mode makes larger drops of varying sizes — an excellent way to simulate marble or granite textures, for example. The paint color can make a transition between two specified colors during the painting stroke. The pencil tool can serve as both a fine airbrush and as a pixel-detailer. The eyedropper selects whatever color it's clicked on, making it the painting color. It's useful for resuming work in an area without searching for a precise color-match in the palette.

PixelPaint offers 1-bit masking. Its visual effects can act on selected regions to even out grainy textures or to blend obvious edges. Valuable effects include Smoothing, which blends the edges of two different color regions to help remove a jagged, stair-step appearance (Figure 28). With grayscale images PixelPaint's smoothing works exceptionally well. Equally valuable is Diffuse, which dithers the edge pixels of two adjoining color areas, creating a somewhat coarse merging of edges, which can subsequently be smoothed. The Sharpen effect can accentuate edges in an image and improve its apparent sharpness. Contrast can be controlled by editing color ranges in the color palette. Brightness can be controlled by darkening or lightening all the values in the palette. Dynamic effects allow distortion of shape and position of an image or part of an image.

Figure 28. Using special efects. PixelPaint's Brush effects can be applied to blend, soften or sharpen edges. And Dynamic Effects provide direct control of effects that seem to change the viewer's perspective.

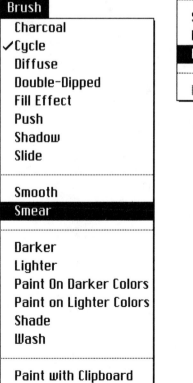

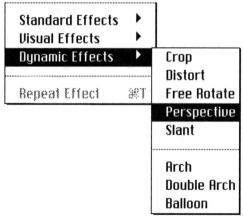

PixelPaint Professional offers all of PixelPaint's tools, and more, in a 16.7 million-color environment that's free from color palette limitations and can produce very soft blends. Its file importation and exportation capabilities include PICT2, TIFF and EPS (Figure 29). With these talents, PixelPaint Professional can be used for illustrative work, image enhancement and retouching of full-color scans. Its masking method system includes the option to view the mask as a paintable and erasable layer. This lets you create or fine-tune the mask with familiar painting tools. Unlike the mask in dedicated 24-

Figure 29. Enhancing images. This image, which began as a scan of a black-and-white photo, was colored and output to film separations for a magazine illustration. Didier Cremieux, a senior artist for the Queens Group, a large New York–based printer, used PixelPaint Professional to produce the special effects in 24-bit color.

bit photo-editing programs, the PixelPaint mask is a yes/no mask. Either paint gets through it, or it doesn't. This limits some of the special effects you can create, but doesn't impede most common editing chores. A convenient slider lets you adjust the transparency of a selection or of the paint that you apply. It can also separate color images. It features extensive separation controls.

Studio/8 is primarily a painting application that's excellent for 256-color work in a variety of file formats and image sizes. Its tool set and navigation controls are powerful and can be learned with little difficulty. In addition to standard painting tools, Studio/8 offers exceptional control over the shape of selections, and it can mask a set of regions that you specify, or it can mask any or all of the 256 colors in the palette. Its interface is perhaps more technical than PixelPaint's, but its tool set is more complete. It has outstanding masking capabilities. You can convert any selected area to a mask and then further refine the shape of the mask. You can mask specific colors or ranges of colors. Its selection tools are powerful, and help you quickly select even intricate areas (Figure 30).

Figure 30. Image editing in Studio/8. Studio/8 has a limited 256-color range, but its tools for selection, transformation, masking and gradients are exceptional. One leaf was auto-selected and cloned several times. The glass was duplicated, tipped and distorted to produce a rounded lip.

Each Studio/8 document has a temporary additional layer onto which you can paint without disturbing the document. This layer is called the Draft Page, and it's an ideal tool for creating a montage. When a chunk of image is in the draft layer, you can freely slide it around over the main image without worrying about disturbing the main image. Paint in the draft layer can have several degrees of transparency (Figure 31).

Studio/8's ability to fill shapes with color gradients is one of its strongest features. Gradients, or transitions from one color to another, are set up by specifying the color of the main bands in a rainbow. You can specify up to 32 individual bands. Usually, you specify a few bands, and Studio/8 automatically adds the right colors in between. The fills can be applied with excellent control of direction, and color spread, and you can select a radiation point for the fill, so that a yellow-to-green fill of an oval shape could have a yellow hotspot anywhere inside the oval that radiates to green in all directions, sensitive to the shape of the oval. This system works well for simulating lighting effects. You can also use various realistic textures as backgrounds or object fills. Studio/8 also works exceptionally well with grayscale images. Another helpful feature is Studio/8's picture preview. This function lets you check to be sure an image is the one you want to open (Figure 32).

Studio/32 expands on the capabilities of Studio/8, in both color depth and the number of useful effects, adding the ability to antialias the edges of new objects and specific areas. The variety of painting, photo-editing and montaging abilities of Studio/32 make it good choice for a broad range of work on bitmapped images (Figure 33). Its basic interface and fundamental feature set are much like Studio/8's but with extensions for 16.7 million colors. Studio/32 works on 32-bit documents on an 8-bit display by dithering 256 colors into approximations of the true colors. Among the key features whose effects are

Figure 31. Studio/8's Goodies. By placing part of an image on Studio/8's Draft Page, you can keep it separate from the pixels of the underlying image, allowing you to edit it and change its transparency before releasing it to become part of the main image.

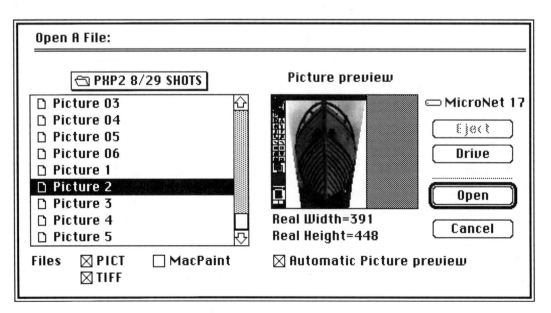

Figure 32. Previewing images. Before you open a PICT, TIFF or MacPaint file in Studio/8, you can identify the image and see its width and height, so that you don't have to wait for a file to open and appear on-screen to find out if it's the image you want.

enhanced by 32-bit color are gradients that don't exhibit color bands nor graininess. Its applied paint can be assigned any degree of transparency. Blending and smudging operations produce smooth boundaries. Its Blur and Sharpen functions give predictable results. In addition to the normal brush, there's a smooth-edged antialiased brush that's a key tool for editing details in photo-retouching. A brush can be a temporary cloning tool for copying one part of the image onto another part, simply by brushing it on. Another powerful brush attribute is the ability to change only the color of a stroked region, rather than its detail. With this capability, you can easily change the color of a flower while keeping its petal textures, highlights and shadows intact.

Studio/32 can open files in the following formats: MacPaint, PICT, TIFF and EPS. It can save images in color or grayscale, PICT, TIFF, EPS and JPEG (special compression) formats. The program uses disk space (or virtual memory) for handling larger images that cannot fit entirely in RAM.

Studio/32's selection abilities are quite powerful. Selectors include a rectangle and a free-form shape. Each tool has the ability to contract around a region, or to expand from within a region. Studio/32 also offers an autoselecting magic wand tool that expands to select areas of similar colors. You can vary its tolerance for similar colors from very similar to very general. Any selection can be automatically traced with the brush, antialiased brush,

Figure 33. Working in Studio/32. Several special effects were applied to this Studio/32 work. The shimmering metallic side pieces are gradient-filled ovals. The bubbles were produced by picking up a circular section and applying spherical distortion. The bubbles were lightened with a semi-transparent fill. For extra depth, a gradient fill was added to the background, which was easily isolated with expanding selection tools.

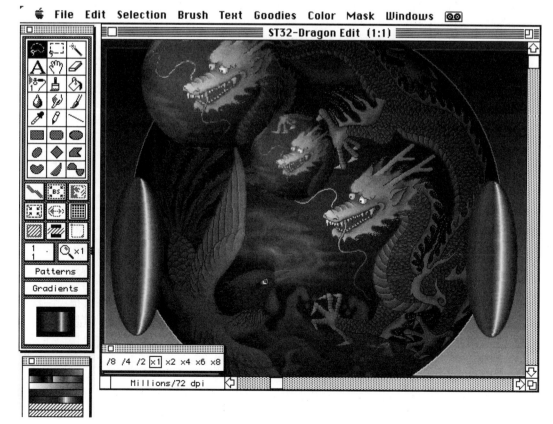

airbrush, water drop or sharpener. The program's masking talents include adding and subtracting selected areas or colors from the mask, which is a 1-bit (protect/affect) type. The shapes of masked regions can be named, saved and retrieved as needed, to save the trouble and time of reselecting areas.

The Studio series provides a way to set up a perspective plane with a vanishing point. Selected areas can automatically be distorted according to their apparent distance along this plane. The perspective plane can also be tiled with multiple copies of a selected area, with each tile properly distorted according to its position on the plane.

Color separators

A number of applications are dedicated to making color separations from the files produced by color image editors. **PrePress Technologies** offers color separation utilities for QuarkXPress, as well as dedicated medium-range and high-end separation programs. QuarkXPress performs four-color separations of its own files based on DCS (or Desktop Color Separation) format, a variant of EPS. A file in DCS format is actually an EPS file composed of five separate files, one for each of the four colors (CMYK) and one PICT preview file. The PICT file is brought into QuarkXPress and manipulated, and at print time QuarkXPress seeks out the four separated files. PhotoMac and Photoshop support DCS as a variant of EPS. In other words, QuarkXPress leaves the sensitive task of color separation to a more specialized program, and then uses Adobe's minimum moiré frequencies and angles to print the separated plates as part of the entire page.

EPS options in Photoshop are extensive. The binary format of PostScript is acceptable in QuarkXPress and takes less space.

PageMaker offers spot color separations only from within the program. However, a page with color TIFF images can be separated using **Aldus**

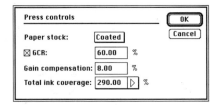

Figure 34. Separating color with Aldus PrePrint. The Aldus PrePrint separation utility provides control of many aspects of film production by imagesetter, including GCR, or gray component replacement.

PrePrint (or **SpectreSeps PM**) (Figure 34), or it can be saved in OPI format for separation in a high-end system (see "Output devices and methods" later in this chapter).

Output devices and methods

For all the emphasis on getting the real world into the computer, we really do run into difficulties trying to get things back out. Output can be in the form of paper, negatives, transparencies or videotape (a truly convenient means of recording, transporting and playing back animations and broadcast images that won't take up gigabytes of hard disk space).

Matching on-screen color to output

TekColor is a utility for the Mac that allows you to match colors on screen to any output device it currently supports (Figure 35). Users are free to create "drivers" for output devices. TekColor resides in the System folder and replaces the standard Macintosh Color Picker. If a particular graphics application does not use the Color Picker, you can't use TekColor. Based on averaged information about various monitors and printers, TekColor allows you to see and compare the available color values of the monitor, printer and full color space, based on a hue bar and color leafs. You can then pick a color available only on the printer, or on both the monitor and printer, and use it in the application with confidence that the color you've chosen will appear on the printed page.

Figure 35. Matching colors. TekColor provides a way to try to ensure that the color an artist sees on the computer screen can be reproduced in print. Other approaches to this color-matching problem include hardware-software calibration devices such as those produced by Radius (for Sony Trinitron monitors) and Barco (for Barco monitors).

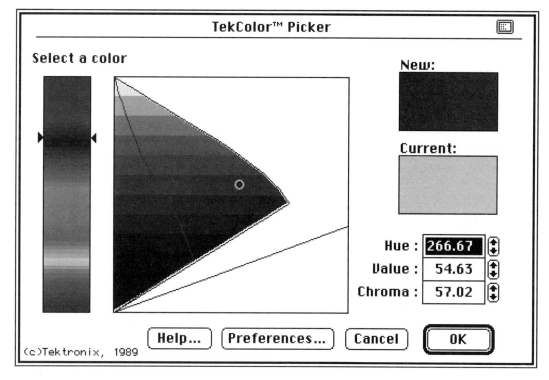

High-resolution laser printers

An alternative to imagesetting to negative film at 1200 to 2540 dpi can be found with high-resolution laser printers, like those made by **Varityper** and **LaserMaster.** This is especially true for halftones to be printed at newspaper quality; a minimum resolution of 1000 dpi prints acceptably at a 60- to 80-line screen.

Figure 36. Producing continuous tone. Although the 4Cast prints at a resolution of 300 dpi, the individual dots can't be detected. This continuous-tone look is produced by varying the amount of heat applied to each dot to control the color intensity and to spread the dots out for solid ink coverage.

Color printers

Although they can't provide proofs that simulate the results of printing as do Chromalins and Matchprints, low-resolution color printers can be very useful for producing comps. **Tektronix** markets a 216-dpi color inkjet printer and a 300-dpi thermal wax transfer printer, both of which can print on various media and use either QuickDraw-based or PostScript-clone drivers. **QMS** markets a 300-dpi color thermal printer with a PostScript interpreter and 35 resident fonts.

An exciting new form of color output device is the continuous-tone color printer. **Du Pont, Kodak** and **Nikon,** and **Iris** and **Fuji** are marketing two different technologies. The Du Pont 4Cast uses dye-sublimation thermal transfer with four dyes to create the equivalent of color photographs at 300 dpi (Figure 36). The result is photographic in quality because the colors are continuous-tone, not dithered as with thermal wax and inkjet printers. It also interprets PostScript and a number of other graphics formats from various platforms. Dye sublimation is a dry process that requires little maintenance, but a special receiver paper must be used. The Iris inkjet printer also produces continuous-tone output at 300 dpi for stunning results, but can print on any kind of paper (Figure 37). For proofing before going to press, this adds one more degree of realism and usefulness.

Film recorders

In many cases, especially for color images, slides are a convenient form of output. Film recorders are of two general types: analog and digital. Analog recorders are also called video printers because they simply intercept the analog RGB signal sent to the monitor and display it on a mini-monitor, which is then photographed. Digital film recorders actually generate the image as a bitmap, usually at 2000 or 4000 horizontal lines. This is also displayed on a miniature monitor and photographed. Digital film recorders in general produce better images but are more expensive and take longer to create slides.

Imagesetters

The field of PostScript-based imagesetters has broadened considerably since the days of the **Linotronic 100.** Linotype itself has improved and expanded its own line. In addition, the **BirmySetter** is a reasonably priced alternative

Figure 37. Outputting large-format sheets. The Iris inkjet printer can provide continuous tone images in formats much larger than most imagesetters and thermal transfer printers.

with a smooth paper transport (actually it prints each page all at once rather than line by line). **Agfa Compugraphic** markets an imagesetter with the powerful Atlas RIP (raster image processor), and Optronics touts the **ColorSetter 2000,** an imagesetter that performs its own screening independent of PostScript, while working transparently with PostScript files. One of the advantages of using an imagesetter is the ability to go directly to film; negatives are desirable for screened images at line-screen frequencies higher than 85 lines per inch.

High-end links

As an alternative to going to your local service bureau and trying your own color separations, some of the high-end prepress vendors offer links to the desktop world (and vice versa). *OPI, open prepress interface,* was instituted by Aldus as a standard format to allow merging of high-resolution scanned files with desktop-produced pages before the pages are output to a separation device. Essentially, OPI is a file format that adds comments to PostScript output. Hell Graphics has endorsed this standard and implemented various desktop links. The latter rasterizes a PostScript page for further manipulation and eventual output on the Scitex. Crosfield has developed its own link called DeskLink, which integrates the page geometry from Ready,Set,Go or DesignStudio with high-resolution scans from one of its scanners. There is some debate about how much time and money are saved using these methods, and whether or not strictly desktop means will eventually produce the same results. Some believe that the results possible on the desktop are already competitive with high-end results. One thing is for sure: If you want to be the judge, you must also be your own production agent.

C H A P T E R   3

Working in Layers

Artist

A pen-and-ink cartoonist by trade, Mike Swartzbeck has been involved in fine art and graphic design on the Macintosh since February 1985, a full six months before Paul Brainerd coined the term *desktop publishing*. In late 1986 his work first appeared in *The MACazine*, where he was a regular illustrator until 1989. In January 1987 he was a featured artist in the premiere issue of *Verbum* magazine, and he has been a regular contributor of print graphics and video/stackware ever since. Two of his pieces were featured in the 1988 MacDaydreams Art Calendar published by Computer Giftware, Inc. of Glendale, California. His work has also been published in *Step-By-Step Electronic Design* newsletter and *Publish* magazine. Swartzbeck is also a regularly featured cartoonist for *Relix*, a Grateful Deadhead "fanzine" published in New York City.

Project

Using a number of ThunderScanned images, I set out to create a lively interplay of textures and effects by employing some advanced layering techniques in Graphic-Works 1.1. I used a Mac Plus with 2.5 MB of RAM, a 20 MB Seagate hard disk drive and ThunderScan version 4. I output proofs and final copies on a LaserWriter.

**PROJECT
OVERVIEW**

A place for bitmaps

I for one still enjoy the pixelated, pointillist look of MacPaint-style bitmaps. They were part of the original Mac aesthetic, and they're a good starting point for someone new to the Mac. I often use a grayscale image as the source material for various dithered bitmaps. As MacPaint format is one of the most basic interpretations of the Mac's screen image, MacPaint images are accessible to owners of any Mac. And printed output will match the screen — true WYSIWYG.

"Flat bitmap" art on the Macintosh offers wide opportunities for experimentation with shadows and textures, allowing me to produce almost impressionistic effects. These opportunities are enhanced through the use of scanners like Koala's MacVision video digitizer and Thunder-Ware's ThunderScan, which uses any ImageWriter as a scanning bed. Scanned images are like my tubes of paint; I can combine various scanned graphics to create the effect I'm seeking.

The components

"Four/Nine" was composed with images saved as MacPaint from ThunderScan, and from MacPaint screen dumps of forms produced by the Moiré CDEV screen saver. It was produced with five separate elements: two versions of the reclining woman, one high-contrast and one with Trace Edges; two versions of a screen-saver dump from Moiré stretched to fill the page, one regular and one with Trace Edges; and a cropped version of a woman's face, stretched to fill about a third of the page.

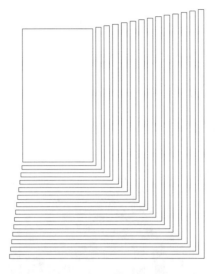

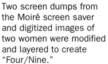
Two screen dumps from the Moiré screen saver and digitized images of two women were modified and layered to create "Four/Nine."

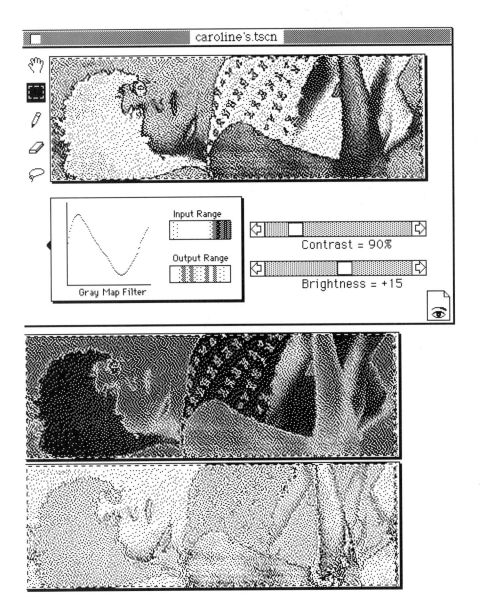

ThunderScan's GrayMap
controls provide numer-
ous possibilities. Using
the pencil tool, I could
manually tweak or en-
tirely redraw the output
waveform controlling to-
nality in various light and
dark areas of the image.

T wo of the source images for "Four/Nine" (the close-up face and the reclining woman) were scanned with ThunderScan (Figure 1). Contrast and brightness were adjusted with the program's slider controls (Figure 2). Then the images were saved in MacPaint format (Figure 3). Two of the source images were then processed with GraphicWorks's transfer mode tools (see "Layered paint environments" on page 65 for a description of the GraphicWorks transfer modes).

The close-up face was imported into GraphicWorks, set to the NotBic transfer mode and dropped over a filled rectangle. The reclining woman was similarly imported, but the transfer mode was set to NotOr. The results of both were saved as separate MacPaint images for use in the final composition.

Assembling the image

Next the treated and untreated images were imported into GraphicWorks and used to build a composite image (Figure 4, a–i). The bottom layer held the shaded image of the reclining woman with the transfer mode set to Copy (a). The next two layers were duplicates of the Moiré screen shot set to NotBic (b) and NotOr (c) modes. Over these went the close-up face set to NotBic (d). Next was the Moiré shot treated with MacPaint's Trace Edges command and placed with the GraphicWorks transfer mode set to Or (e). These are followed

Figure 1. Making the scan. A newly scanned image was saved in Thunder-Scan's native format for editing.

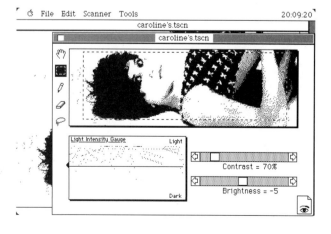

Figure 2. Adjusting contrast and brightness. The slider bars at the lower right of the ThunderScan window were used to set contrast and brightness, tested in a small, selected area of the editing window.

Layered paint environments

In spite of major advances in bitmap paint software, many of the tools still closely resemble those of the classic MacPaint, albeit with major alterations and upgrades — MacPaint's spray can, for instance, became an elegant, fully functional airbrush with widely varying settings in programs like GraphicWorks, ComicWorks and Electronic Arts' Studio/1. The easily identifiable paint tools, in contrast to the rather esoteric palettes in some PostScript illustrating applications shorten the learning time for any paint program.

Anyone who has used a Mac long enough to learn MacPaint tools will already have a headstart on learning most of the second- and third-generation paint environments. Most of the "tricks" learned in MacPaint carry over almost completely. However, multilayer paint programs offer the advantage of controlling the way images interact with layers of pixels "beneath" them. Shown here are six images treated with the transfer modes of GraphicWorks and placed over a light-medium gray background.

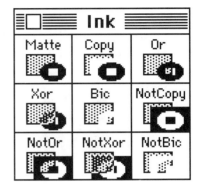

Or: White pixels turn clear and allow the layer beneath to show through.

NotOr: Black pixels turn clear, allowing the layer beneath to show through, and white ones turn black and obscure any layer beneath.

Bic: White pixels turn clear, allowing the layer beneath to show through, and black ones turn white, obscuring any layer beneath.

NotBic: Black pixels turn clear and allow the layer beneath to show through.

Xor: White pixels turn clear, allowing the layer beneath to show through, and black pixels reverse any pixels beneath them, turning black to white and white to black.

NotXor: Black pixels turn clear, allowing the layer beneath to show through, and white pixels reverse any pixels beneath them, turning black to white and white to black.

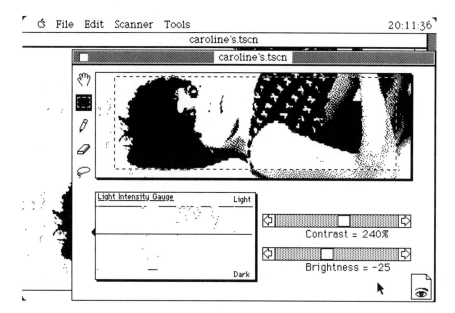

Figure 3. Finalizing the effect. When an optimal setting had been achieved by selecting a portion of the image (shown here) and experimenting with it, Select All was used to adjust the entire image to the new settings. The image was then saved as a MacPaint file.

Figure 4 (opposite). Layering the images. The nine treated and untreated images were layered in Graphic-Works. The progressive development of the "Four/Nine" image is shown in steps (a) through (i).

by two more copies of the reclining woman treated with Trace Edges, again set to Or (f, g), and another copy of the Moiré shot with treated Trace Edges and set to Or (h). (The three sets of edge-traced images were used here to keep the composition from becoming weak or busy from line work that was too thin.) On top of all these stacked elements was a copy of the edge-traced reclining woman with transfer mode Bic to give the image more dimensionality and to help separate the reclining woman's image from the rest of the background (i).

After I had tweaked the image to my taste, it was saved both in Graphic-Works's native format (CBOK) and as a MacPaint file. The GraphicWorks version was archived with StuffIt, and the MacPaint version was saved on disk, for use in a magazine and for easier uploading to my user group BBS — the MacPaint file is smaller than the same image stored in the GraphicWorks format, and anyone who owns a Mac can look at MacPaint files.

In retrospect

The Mac graphics field seems to be dominated by PostScript and 32-bit color. But there is certainly a future in bitmapped graphics in the areas of fine art, illustration, and video and interface design for graphic hypermedia applications such as HyperCard and SuperCard.

Along with brightness, contrast and gray map adjustments, programs like ImageStudio offer a host of effects such as diffusion, sharpening, softening and blurring (producing lush, undulating bitmap textures), and allow the resulting images to be saved as dithered bitmaps as well as in the standard grayscale formats. Hence, the sophistication of grayscale editing can be used to create even more sophisticated MacPaint images. I didn't really need to employ such techniques in this piece, but they are becoming a standard part of my overall approach to manipulating flat bitmaps.

a

b

c

d

e

f

g

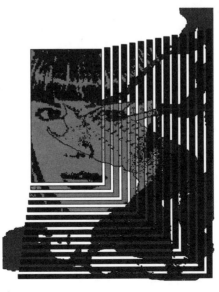

h

i

Mike Swartzbeck

"The myth that computers will take away artists' work could be a self-fulfilling prophecy, really; if you don't try to make the time to explore and learn how to handle the new media, then you're going to be left behind. My only fear of computers was the fear that I might be left behind because I couldn't get at one and learn how to use it soon enough."

Escape was composed of photos digitized with Thunder-Scan, with effects and assembly done in MacPaint 1.5.

Beyond the Temple was made from images saved in ThunderScan format, opened in Image-Studio and heavily modified using its filtering and graymap controls, and saved in MacPaint format for use in Graphic-Works. Once assembled, the final GraphicWorks composition was saved in MacPaint format, placed in PageMaker and resized down to increase the resolution to 150 dots per inch (as were all the images on this spread).

Atlas Escapes was composed of photos digitized with MacScan software driving a Princeton L300 sheet-fed scanner. Effects and assembly were accomplished in GraphicWorks 1.1.

CHAPTER 4

With a Little Imagination...

Designer

Mike Uriss works as a designer, illustrator and art director in San Diego. He currently uses Macintosh and IBM computers for publishing and industrial video production. Having studied at the Art Institute and the Academy of Art in Chicago, Uriss has strong fine art leanings that are demonstrated in this project.

Project

Since I'm from the Midwest, surfing was one of the first things to catch my eye when I came to San Diego. I wanted to depict the surfing scene in an unusual way, in contrast to the typical handling of visuals relating to the sport (which could be characterized as "dayglo pop"). I was more interested in the idea of illusion than in pop iconography. The "Eye Surf" image tends to ask: "Is she a figment of his imagination or vice versa?"

The piece was produced on a Mac II with 2 MB of RAM, the Apple 13-inch color monitor and 8-bit video card, and was proofed on a LaserWriter Plus. A limited edition of final printouts were output on a Linotronic 300 imagesetter.

The creative process

In many examples of creating fine art, the finished piece may not be completely envisioned from the start. In this case, for example, I started with existing images and a notion. I had a suspicion that the popular image of surfing (dayglo colors and blondes on the beach) might be misleading, and that underneath it all there might be a purpose, or some kind of spiritual benefit to be derived from riding the waves. At least that's how I felt after talking with some of the older surfers I met on the beach, who for the most part were steadfast in their conviction that their sport brought them one-on-one with Mother Nature.

Mother Nature in the waves was one of the initial images that formed in my mind, and my artistic affinity to surrealist painters helped this image along. Part of the beauty of being able to scan images into the computer is that they supply raw material. The task of the artist then becomes one of working with the images to find a harmony among them and to express a notion, or to carry out the original spark of inspiration.

The technical process

This piece took full advantage of an early release of ImageStudio. The idea was to isolate all the various elements from their original photos and bring them together in a semi-realistic picture with a fantastic twist. I used portions of different portraits but tried to maintain optimal tonal values and a degree of realism. It's quite possible to overdo the editing in programs like ImageStudio, and to lose some of the most valuable parts of scanned images, such as textures.

Parts of four images were combined to form the EyeSurf montage. This image of a woman's face was suitable because of its pose and dramatic shading.

The surfer was sort of a stock image showing a characteristic moment in the activity of surfing.

The image of a
woman's hair was
central to the compo-
sition and to the idea
of creating an image
of Mother Nature
from the waves.

An image of waves
was scanned,
cropped and scaled.

started with images of three different women and the surfer, which I had selected for their creative potential and quality of highlight and shadow. These images were tightly cropped and scanned on a Sharp flatbed scanner at 100 percent of their original size at a resolution of 75 dpi (see pages 72 and 73).

Perfecting the pieces

First the unneeded portions of the separate images were "opaqued out" with pure white. A brush-stroke technique was used to suggest the effect of splashing waves in the case of the surfer (Figure 1).

Then the scan of hair was selected with the selection rectangle and inverted (a negative of the image was made). My intention was to make the hair appear translucent, as if the light source was behind it (Figure 2). ▮ *Throughout the entire editing process an inverted image can still be modified with the graymap editor (at the bottom of the tool menu) in order to adjust contrast, balance of values and directional movement. This ease of manipulation is one of the benefits of using grayscale images.*

Zooming in on the face section revealed the arrangement of grayscale information within the pixels. For the sake of contrast and effect, only half of the face was "touched up" with ImageStudio's blending tools (Figure 3). ▮ *For producing smooth effects ImageStudio provides retouching tools such as the "water drop" and "finger," which, used in different ways, can average the grayscale information over a broad area of pixels. Specifically the water drop tool blends existing values in a radial direction, and the finger tool smears value in the direction in which it is dragged.*

Figure 1. Modifying the surfer. The splashing waves were enhanced with white brush strokes. **Note:** This and other step-by-step images shown in this chapter were re-created from prints of the original scans, which had not been saved on disk.

In addition to smoothing the surface of the face and shoulder, I added highlights of pure white in the lower chin area. These highlights were then smoothed with the same combination of tools as before. The paintbrush was used to block in important areas along the bottom of the image (Figure 4). Different-sized brush strokes were selected from the pen palette (below the tool palette).

For the purpose of resizing, the surfer image was selected with the selection rectangle and copied to the clipboard. A straight line was then drawn from corner-to-corner of the original selection by holding the Shift key while using

Figure 2. Illuminating the hair. Inverting the hair made it look like it was lit from behind.

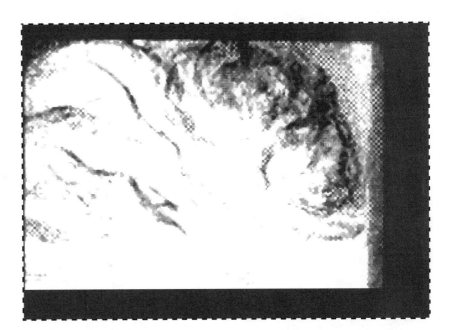

Figure 3. Editing the face. Half of the face was smeared and blended to give it a liquid quality.

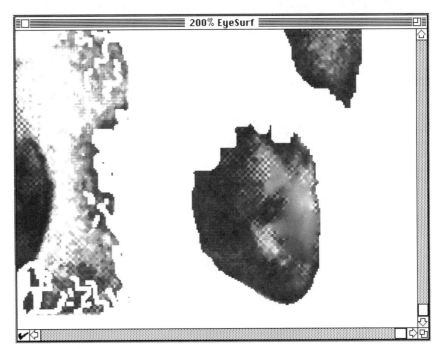

the pencil tool (Figure 5). To ensure proportional scaling of the surfer image a new selection rectangle was created along the pencil line. The image on the clipboard was then pasted into the new selection, and ImageStudio made it automatically conform to the selection rectangle (Figure 6).

Putting the parts together

Now the pieces were ready to go together. From this point on, much of the manipulation involved blending and smoothing the transitions between

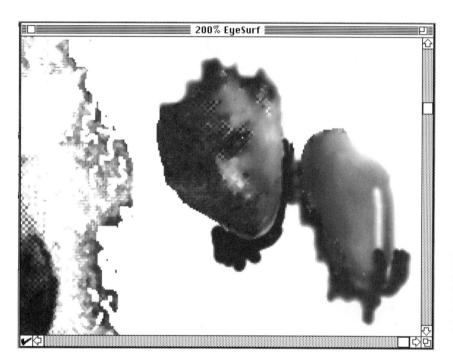

Figure 4. Confining the image. After the face and shoulder were smoothed, highlights were added to the chin and light areas were blocked in with dark brush strokes.

Figure 5. Setting up for resizing. After the surfer was selected and copied, a diagonal pencil line was drawn to help determine a proportionally smaller selection rectangle.

Figure 6. Putting in the surfer. Pasting the surfer image into a smaller selection rectangle automatically reduced the image.

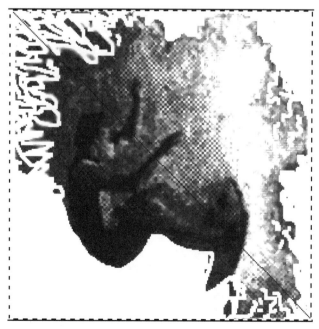

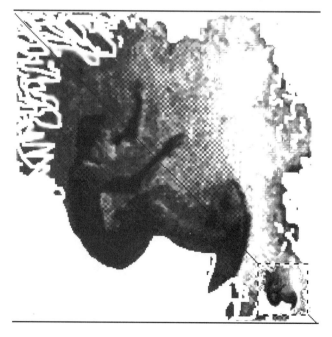

different parts of the image. First the surfer was positioned and the edges of the two images were smoothed with the finger and water drop tools. Rotate Page Left was used to flip a copy of the hair in the direction I needed for use as an area of blended hair and water on the side of the face.

Then I touched up certain areas of the image with the paintbrush, opting to paint only on darker shades using the settings shown in Figure 7. The effect of these settings is that "paint" will be applied only to the areas that are darker than the current shade (the selection in the Current Shade box in the Shades palette).

The hair had to be scaled in the same manner as the surfer. Then it was positioned and its edges were blended using the finger and water drop tools (Figure 8).

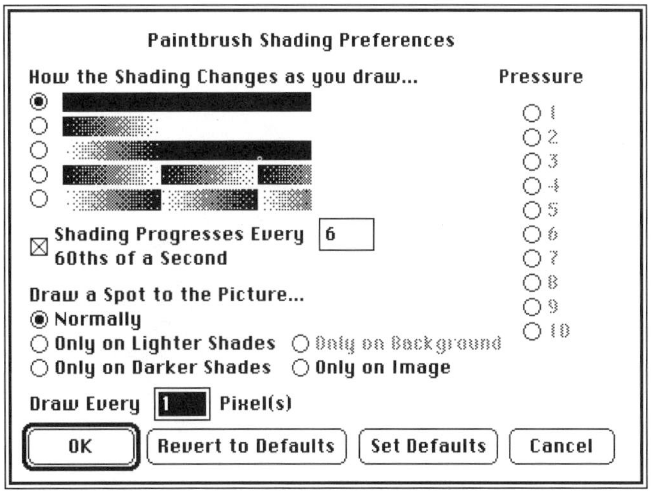

Figure 7. Specifying paintbrush preferences. The paintbrush was set to paint on darker shades only.

Figure 8. Putting the hair and water in place. Selective painting, then rotating and sizing were performed on the blended hair/water before putting it in place.

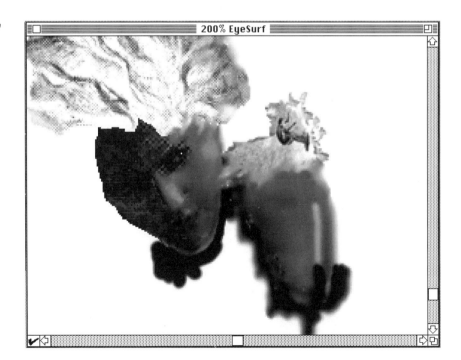

Playing with water

Of course, an image like this needed some real water. I opened an image of waves and cropped and scaled it (Figure 9). Obviously the edges needed to be smoothed, and again the water drop and finger tools were employed.

After "feathering" the edges of the waves, I decided to put back some of the highlights that the diffusing, or smoothing, process had taken away, by adding pure white and then smoothing the edges until I finally arrived at the effect I wanted (Figure 10). The last major effect was the result of duplicating and rotating a section of hair, which I then modeled as though it were metamorphosing from hair to water (Figure 11).

The finishing touches

Only a few final touches remained. Painting and smoothing pure white produced a soft look and suggested the formation of water droplets (Figure

Figure 9. Adding the water. Fortunately, the scan of water was full of turbulence and highlights.

Figure 10. Re-working the water. Too much detail was lost in smoothing, so white highlights were reintroduced and worked in.

12). ▮ *More attention to detail can be achieved by zooming to 400 percent. However, this kind of pixel editing can also become tedious.*

In retrospect

By using grayscale image-editing processes, I achieved my initial goal of creating a fantasy setting with real-life images — and captured a little bit of Southern California romanticism in the process. On the one hand, the piece can be seen as a bit of whimsy, and on the other as a surrealist exploration of the true surfing experience.

Figure 11. Adding more hair/water. Copying and rotating a section of hair provided raw material for a transition between hair and water.

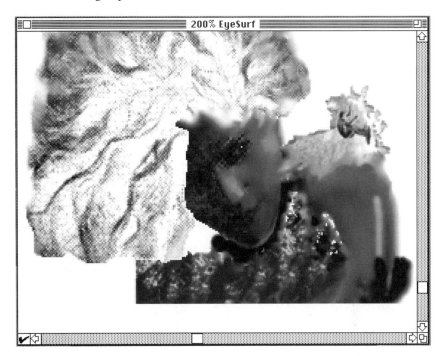

Figure 12. Implying water droplets. Final highlights were added at 400 precent to suggest water drops.

PORTFOLIO

Mike Uriss

"In the beginning, using a mouse to render an image felt a little like drawing with an unopened box of crayons. However, the more familiar I became with desktop publishing tools, the less cumbersome it became, and now I feel like I have the use of a hybrid electronic stat camera, drawing board, easel, photo-retouching and type-setting device all in the palm of my hand.

"I find computer graphics a time-saving and 'brave new' medium. How much time do graphic artists waste shooting repetitious photostats and retouching negatives? How much time do fine artists waste mixing paints, stretching and applying gesso to canvas and cleaning brushes? How many times have you found an artist taping up X-acto knife wounds? No more glue, no more scissors, no more dull pencils and no more paint-spattered clothes.

"New software development like the photo-retouching programs has given me the opportu-nity to digitize via the video camera and flatbed scanner, and to experiment with various design solutions before outputting to comprehensive, camera-ready art or final pieces.

"I can't really say enough about the possibili-ties of computer-generated art, so allow me to paraphrase James Brown: 'Computer graphics are on the scene . . . like a sex machine.'"

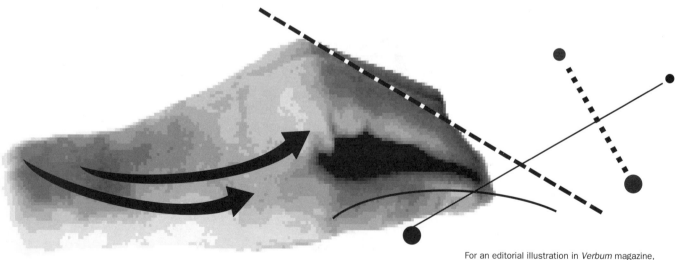

For an editorial illustration in *Verbum* magazine, I used a low resolution TIFF image from a video scan and added geometric elements to convey a contrast between drawing by hand and drawing by computer.

Eerie Eric (opposite page), a color portrait, was heavily posterized using the brightness and contrast tools in Adobe Photoshop.

Quad Portrait (left), illustrating various painting and retouching effects, was developed in Image-Studio from a Mac-Vision video scan.

This cassette cover for Castle Door Music, a Southern California writing and recording company, was done in Photo-shop (the text was created in FreeHand).

CHAPTER 5

A Martian Christmas Card

Designer

John Knoll is a Visual Effects Supervisor at Industrial Light & Magic (ILM), the special-effects division of Lucasfilms, which won the 1989 Visual Effects Oscar for *The Abyss*. While attending film school at USC, he became involved in model-making and, shortly thereafter, motion-control systems. He is also a software developer and was a codeveloper of Photoshop.

Project

This image was created as a Christmas card for the special-effects crew of a feature film called *Spaced Invaders,* from Touchstone Pictures.

The card was produced with a Macintosh II with 5 MB of RAM, a Rodime 140 MB hard disk drive, a RasterOps 264 24-bit display card, an Apple 13-inch RGB monitor, a Microtek MSF-300Z flatbed scanner, and a custom laser output device at ILM. Adobe Photoshop was used for all of the retouching.

PROJECT OVERVIEW

A personal gesture

While I was looking at my wedding album, I saw a group shot of the friends with whom I had worked on the special effects for the film *Spaced Invaders*. I decided I would turn that innocent photo into a humorous Christmas card using Photoshop.

The idea was to alter the heads and faces of the people in the photograph to make them look like the martians from the film. This involved making their heads much bigger — with huge foreheads, but tiny little faces — as well as making the skin color just the right shade of green and adding antennae.

Photoshop tools that were used to turn the photo below into an assemblage of martians included (clockwise from upper left) the rubber stamp tool (for cloning parts of the image to paint over other parts), the smudge tool (for blending away the "seams" of pasted-in images), the eyedropper (for picking up a particular color from the image to use as paint) and the paintbrush (used in various sizes to create new forms, highlights and shadows).

This is the original image, a group shot of the special-effects crew of *Spaced Invaders*, the motion picture, as they appeared in real life at my wedding.

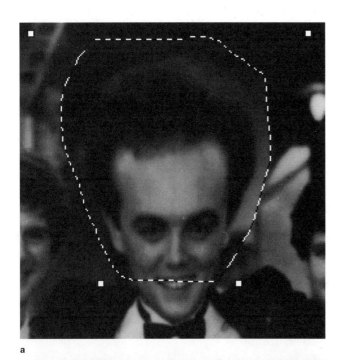

a

Shown here are the
three major phases
of the project: First,
enlarging the fore-
head (a), then pinch-
ing the face (b), and
finally, coloring the
skin and adding
antennae (c).

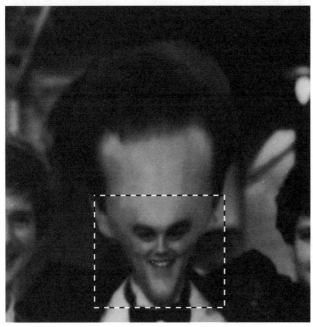

b

c

n December 1989, I decided that I wanted to send a different kind of Christmas card to the friends who had worked on *Spaced Invaders* with me. A few months earlier, they had all attended my wedding, where a group photo had been taken.

Scanning

A friend of mine had just bought a Microtek 24-bit flatbed scanner, so I began by taking a 5 x 7-inch print of the photo and a bunch of floppies over to his home. I knew that ultimately I wanted to reproduce the image as 4 x 6-inch photographic prints and that 200 pixels per inch was a pretty good resolution for my purposes. This left me with a horizontal resolution of at least 1200 pixels (6 inches x 200 pixels per inch) for the input scan.

The Microtek scanning DA can be set for 200 dpi, but a test scan showed some funny interpolation artifacts at this resolution. I've noticed that other scanners do this too, so I've cultivated the habit of scanning everything at 300 dpi, and then resizing the image down in Photoshop.

I scanned the photo and saved it as a TIFF file. Then I launched Photoshop and opened the file. Using the Resample command, I resized it down to a width of 6 inches at 200 dpi. The image was then about 2.8 MB. I saved it onto four floppies using StuffIt and headed home.

Color correcting the image

After bringing the scan home, I loaded it onto my hard disk. First I had to adjust brightness, contrast and color balance. I find Photoshop's Adjust Levels control to be the best tool for doing all these things at once. The scan looked a little dark and a little yellow, so I boosted the gamma (or distribution of color values) of the whole image a little and brightened the blue channel a little more to counteract the yellow cast (Figure 1).

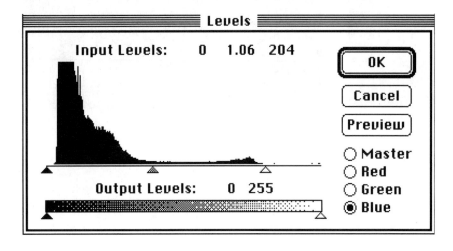

Figure 1. Adjusting gamma and color. Gamma can be thought of as brightness and contrast over the color range. It was adjusted first for the whole image and then for the blue color range only.

Enlarging the head

My friend Patrick, with his already expansive forehead, was my first victim. First, I set the feather edge of the lasso tool to a radius of 1 pixel and selected just his face. I copied this to the clipboard because I was going to need it again later (Figure 2).

I selected the upper half of Pat's head using the lasso tool and made a floating copy of it by holding down the Option key and dragging the selection up a pixel or two (Figure 3). Using the Perspective command (from Image, Effects), I stretched his head up and out, giving it just the right proportions for a proper martian (Figure 4).

Figure 3. Making a floating copy of the upper head. Option-dragging the selection a pixel or two created a copy of the upper part of the head.

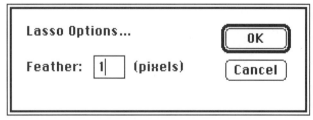

Figure 2. Copying the face. A lassoed selection with a little feathering was used to copy the face to the clipboard. Feathering creates a small border of blurring around the selection, so it blends more naturally with the background it will be pasted into.

While the distorted copy was still floating, I trimmed away the background that had been selected with the head. When I was happy with the closely cropped image, I put it down by clicking outside it. ❚ *Using the lasso tool while holding down the Command key, you can carve pieces off a selection. If the selection is a copy or a floating selection, those pieces that are carved off are in effect deleted.*

Using the rubber stamp tool, I cloned the forehead area and painted out the eyes, which had become stretched (Figure 5). Finally, I fixed the seams left by the rubber stamp by using the smudge tool.

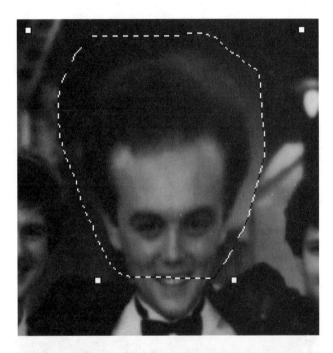

Figure 4. Stretching the head. The Perspective command was used to enlarge the head.

Figure 5. Extending the forehead by cloning. The forehead was extended down to the nose. This left seams, which were then eliminated with the smudge tool.

Replacing the original face

Next, I pasted the original face that was on the clipboard back into the image (Figure 6) and again touched up the seam with the smudge tool (Figure 7).

Since martians have smaller-than-normal faces on larger-than-normal heads, the next step was to shrink the bottom part of his head. The Pinch plug-in filter provided an easy way to do this. Using a selection rectangle, I selected the area that I wanted to squeeze, and then selected Pinch from the filter menu. I tried a couple of values, but found that 65 percent looked the best (Figure 8).

Figure 6. Replacing the face. The copy of the face on the clipboard was pasted back in.

Figure 7. Smoothing the seams. The smudge tool was used again to make the union seamless.

Adjusting the skin color

Getting just the right green skin color was critical in achieving the true martian look. I approached this by selecting just the skin areas with the lasso tool. Since the hairline at the top of his head is a gradual transition, the selection mask needed to be soft in those areas. I did this by first selecting the lower edges of his face with the lasso tool's feather radius set to 1, then changing the feather to 5 and adding the upper edges to the selection. Since I didn't want to change the eyes or mouth, I set the feather back to 1 and cut these areas out of the selection. ▌ *Holding down the Shift key when making a selection adds to the current selection.*

A white silhouette was left selected (Figure 9). I then used the Adjust Levels command to perform the color adjustment, darkening down the red and blue channels until the color looked right.

Painting antennae

No martian is complete without his antennae, so the next step was to paint a set of them. I picked up the color from Pat's forehead using the eyedropper, and then drew the basic shapes with the paintbrush. With a smaller brush, I added highlights and shadows to make the antennae more three-dimensional (Figure 10).

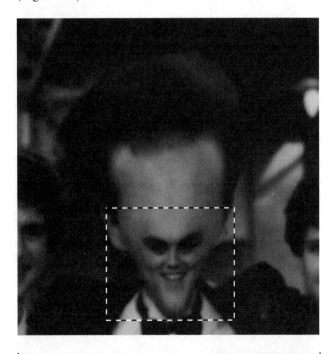

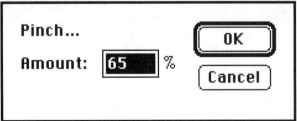

Figure 8. Pinching the face. The Pinch filter set to 65 percent sufficiently shrank the middle portion of the selection, as if it had been pinched.

Finishing the card

The modification process was repeated for everyone else in the image. I then used a custom film recorder at ILM to print the image onto a Kodak 35mm color negative and had a local one-hour photo facility make the prints. The laser output device at ILM produces a finer result, but an acceptable image could be had with an Agfa Matrix slide writer. The card looked just like a snapshot and went over quite well.

John Knoll

"I've always had a love of hobbies, but my hobbies have the strange habit of becoming professions. Every time this happens I have to find a new hobby to replace the one that became a job.

"I first got involved with computers when I was a professional model-maker (you guessed it, model-making had formerly been a hobby). I taught myself programming and designed a four-channel motion-control system on an Apple II. This led to a job as a motion-control camera operator, so I began to dabble in image processing and computer graphics. The next thing you know, my brother Tom and I were at work on a program that eventually became Photoshop. At the moment, I'm not sure what my next hobby will be."

Figure 9. Coloring the skin green. Feathering can be set differently for different parts of the same selection. The skin of the face was selected to be turned green. Changing the amount of feathering to 5 gave a softer edge to the selection at the hairline.

Figure 10. Painting the antennae. Color from the forehead was picked up with the eyedropper and used to paint a pair of antennae with the paintbrush.

CHAPTER 6

Sculpting with Masks

Designer

Peter Vanags studied fine art and marine biology at the University of California at Berkeley. He has applied his technical and artistic skills to such areas as desktop publishing and illustration, PostScript programming, graphic design, and multimedia and computer interface design since 1985. His current emphasis is in Macintosh color prepress techniques, and color/grayscale image scanning and retouching. The founder and president of Electronic Ink, a San Francisco design and consulting firm, he is also a contributor to *Publish* magazine and *Step-By-Step Electronic Design* newsletter.

Project

I created this marbled effect as part of an exploration of design options for use in the Taubman Companies' desktop-published print materials. At the same time that I was trying to create the appearance that their corporate logo was etched out of marble, I was also trying to develop a set of procedures that could easily be applied to any scanned graphic (type, for example). The original marble texture was from a slide of a statue with marble next to it, taken by Michael Everitt.

I used a Macintosh II with 5 MB of RAM, a Radius 19-inch color monitor with 8-bit color card, a MicroNet 45 MB removable hard disk drive, and a Barneyscan slide scanner with an early version of Photoshop software, at that time called BarneyscanXP. The entire project was developed in 8-bit mode, even though the marble was scanned in 24-bit color.

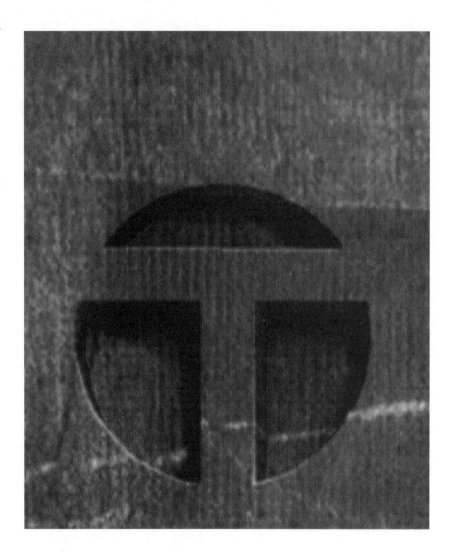

PROJECT OVERVIEW

Design goals

At the time of this project, the Barney-scanXP (or Photoshop) software had a multitude of features, but no one really knew what its potential was as an artistic tool. One purpose of the project was to see if the application could produce the effect of a shape etched in marble. Not only could it handle the task, but it convinced me it deserved to become the tool of choice for editing and manipulating digitized images. Additionally, my experiments with Photoshop's sophisticated calculation tools produced some unexpected but appealing results, such as a whitewash effect.

Design process

I had used the Photoshop software before, but only to mask, sharpen, despeckle and gamma-correct scanned grayscale images. Since I had done this to well over a hundred grayscale images, I was relatively comfortable with the software, but I hadn't explored the mysterious, sophisticated Calculate pop-up menu. At the time, the software was in beta form and had only the sketchiest of manuals, which glossed rapidly over these functions. In trying to create the effect of a logo etched from marble, I would try to learn what all these complicated functions did while at the same time trying to complete a real project.

When I began work on the marble logo, I thought that simply darkening the stone in the logo's shape would produce a convincing carved effect. But once I had done this, I realized that creating a realistic etched-stone effect required considerably more than just darkening. The image looked like a flat piece of marble stained dark in the shape of a logo; it conveyed no depth at all.

To make the image look more convincing, I tried offsetting the marble texture in the sections that made up the recessed

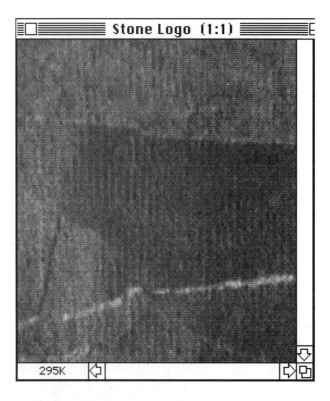

The original marble background was a nondescript, neutral color. So the first thing I did was adjust the color balance of the midtones (medium tonal values) and highlights (lighter tonal values) to achieve a more interesting green tint.

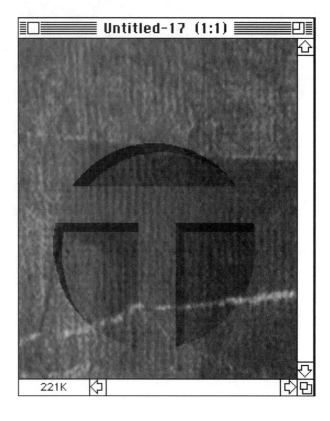

After imprinting the marble with the basic logo shape, I realized that it lacked depth and realism.

portion of the etched-out area. I hoped this would make the etched areas appear as a separate plane behind the main surface of the marble. While offsetting the stone texture helped, it only looked a little convincing, and only along the sections where veins ran across the marble. In the rest of the image, the offset of the texture was much too subtle to notice.

To strengthen the effect of the offset marble texture, I began distorting the sides of the etched area, so the texture would appear to "flow" down the sides of the etched area to the bottom. After a considerable amount of time copying, pasting, stretching and skewing little rectangles of marble texture, the image still didn't look right. It still seemed too subtle and sketched-in; it lacked the strength and boldness of a shape etched in marble.

At this point, I went back to the original masks I had used to darken the marble in the shape of the logo in the first place and reapplied them to darken the most shadowy areas of the image again. Now the image of the logo was bolder, but somehow still lacked realism.

The final step in bringing the image to life was creating internal shadows for the etched section, using the airbrush and blending tools to create shadow shapes. It's interesting to note that the most freeform and painterly procedure that I used on the image also made the biggest difference in terms of its realism. After a few final touches of white airbrush to add highlights on the front edges of the logo, it was practically complete.

Scanning
Scanning with Barneyscan was very easy, due to the QuickScan 35 module, which installs itself on Photoshop's File menu and allows direct access to the scanner.

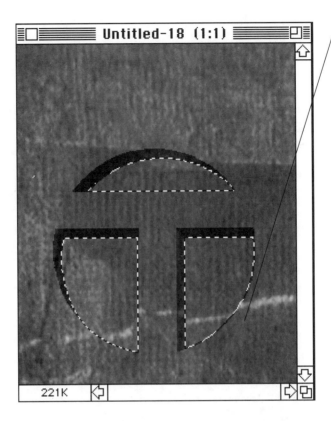

To add realism, I tried offsetting the recessed part of the logo. Where veins ran across the logo, this technique helped somewhat.

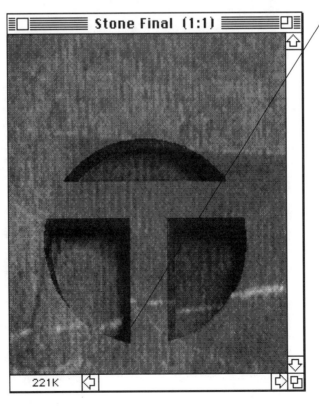

The final touch of realism required a painterly hand to simulate the gradual shading that would be likely to occur across the logo.

The concept of *channels* is key to using Photoshop. A channel is like an image layer. In the typical RGB file, there is a channel for RGB together, and a channel for each of the three colors. These are numbered 0 through 3. You can add more channels in 8-bit grayscale; these are called *alpha channels*. Since these alpha channels can interact with the original image in highly flexible ways, it's possible to create a series of masks and combine each with the original image to modify it selectively and with a particular effect. In this project, there are two masks. The first was combined with the original image twice, and the second was used once. ▌ *By thinking through from the start how many effects you need, you can avoid the mistake of creating too many masks and adding unnecessary steps to the process.*

The first mask

Figure 1 shows the first mask, a three-dimensional letter T created with three different grays. This is the basic shape of the logo, which was combined with the marble to create the underlying embossed look. ▌ *It's important that each gray area is composed of a single, distinct shade, since the magic wand tool enables you to select an extended area of the same color with a single click.*

Since white is opaque and black is transparent in Photoshop, I inverted the mask just drawn and "subtracted" it from the marble image (Figure 2). ▌ *Calculations like Subtract offer many potential effects, not all of which are obvious right away. Sometimes you simply have to try some different options to determine which effect you need.*

Figure 1. Painting the logo shape. This three-dimensional "T" was painted by hand with three distinct grays. It would act like a cookie cutter, first for quickly stamping the marble three-dimensionally, and then for shifting the recessed portion of the new logo.

Figure 2. Inverting the logo. Now mostly transparent, the logo was ready to be "subtracted" from the marble.

```
Subtract...                    OK
   Source 1: Stone Logo      Cancel
   Channel: RGB
   Source 2: Stone Logo
   Channel: #4
     Scale: 1
    Offset: 0
Destination: New
   Channel: New
```

Subtraction left most of the marble as it was — this was important, because it was already color-corrected — and selectively darkened the areas underneath the lighter parts of the mask. Photoshop would use each level of gray for its corresponding transparency; since white is opaque, the lighter grays are more opaque than the darker grays.

Subtraction was performed several times before an acceptable new image was created (Figure 3). ▌*Photoshop's Calculate functions are a major source of its power. Sometimes they require a little trial and error, but they allow you to accomplish just about anything. In addition, they let you combine channels of two different files or of the same file and create a new file with the result. This way, you can create several versions and compare them, without changing the source images.*

In between tries the gray levels of the mask were tweaked via the Adjust Input Levels window. Finally, the desired shading was achieved (Figure 4). This concluded the first combination of the first mask with the marble.

To add another degree of realism, I decided to use a slightly offset portion of the marble for the recessed part of the logo. In other words, the sunken-in base of the logo would in fact look somewhat shifted. ▌*If a smooth material without a lot of texture and veins were used, this step would not be necessary.*

To achieve the offset, I returned to the original file, inverted the mask back to normal and used the magic wand to select the gray areas corresponding to the recessed part of the logo (Figure 5). ▌*To add other areas to a magic wand selection, hold down the Shift key.*

Figure 3. Using Calculate functions. The Subtract dialog box gives an indication of the options available through the Calculate functions. You can request that the result be put into a new file and keep the source file "as is."

Figure 4. Making the first stamp. As a result of several applications of Subtract and adjustments of grayscale masks, the logo was embossed in the marble.

Figure 5. Selecting the back of the logo. Because the recesssed part of the original image was a single gray shade (see Figure 1), the entire area could be selected with one click of the magic wand.

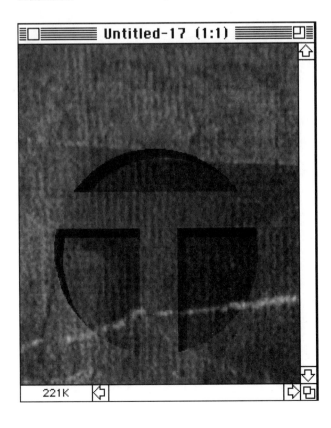

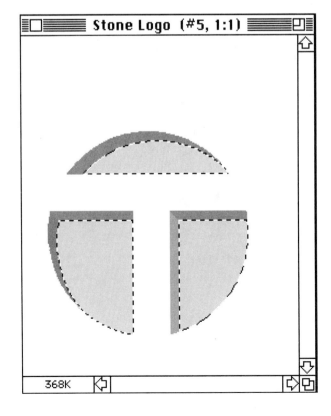

Even after I switched channels, the selection showed through, so I could switch to the RGB channel to see what part of the marble now corresponded to the bottom of the logo. Another feature of Photoshop allows you to move the selection boundaries by holding down the Command and Option keys and dragging within a selection area. This moves the selection boundaries, without displacing portions of the image they select. Using this technique, I was able to drag the selection boundaries up and to the left a short distance (Figure 6). I then selected Copy.

All this, remember, was happening in the original file. I clicked on the new file (the result of the subtraction described earlier) and pasted in the copied parts of the original marble. I dragged these into place, exactly covering the darkened areas that represented the recessed part of the logo (Figure 7). Now the back of the logo was properly shifted. With the areas still selected, I adjusted brightness to darken them (Figure 8). A click outside the selected areas locked them in place. The embossed look was now even more realistic.

The second mask

I wasn't going to stop there, though. At this point the shadows were too well-defined, and the edges were too sharp. First, I wanted the inside of the logo to have a more gradual shading, so I created a new mask based on the first.

Back on the old file, I selected the same areas representing the recessed part of the logo in channel 4 and created a new channel. The selection shows through in the new channel as it would in any other channel. ∎ *Another*

Figure 6. Shifting the selection. Option-Command-drag moved just the selection boundaries.

Figure 7. Copying and pasting. The pasted areas from the original file had to be dragged into place on the Subtracted image.

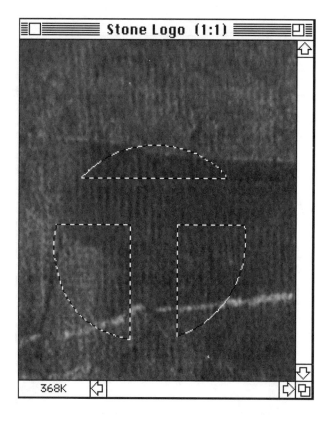

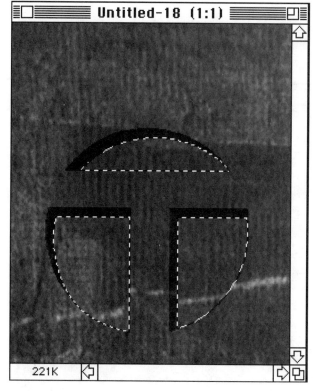

convenient feature of Photoshop is that any painting done in a channel with a selected area will be masked by the selection.

Selecting a medium gray, I used the paintbrush within the selected areas to create the shading I desired. The selection boundaries cleanly cut off the brush strokes. The fingertip tool was also applied to thin out the shading (Figure 9). ▮ *Using the feathering option of the lasso selection tool, you can have the paintbrush strokes gradually fade away as they approach the selection boundaries.*

As I did with the first mask, I then inverted this mask and subtracted it from the RGB channel of the new file. This darkened the back of the logo again, but in a smoother and more gradual fashion (Figure 10).

The finishing touches

A few more techniques were used to finish this project. Due to the shifting of the recessed part of the logo, one of the veins in the marble was now strangely broken. This was quickly fixed by using a rectangular selection to isolate the right side of the upright of the T, copying it by Option-dragging and moving the copy back into place, and then skewing the selection until the vein was rejoined. ▮ *Using a copy on top of the original ensures there will be no background showing through after a skewing operation.*

Then I added streaks of highlights with the airbrush tool. ▮ *Shift-clicking allows you to brush in a straight line.*

Figure 8. Darkening. The selected areas were darkened before they were set down.

Figure 9. Making the second mask. The work of the paintbrush and fingertip tools was sharply masked by the selection boundaries.

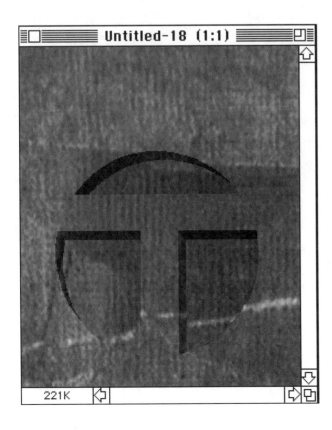

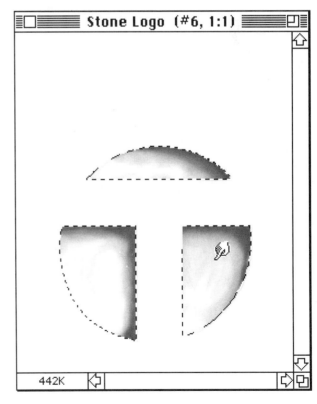

The image was almost what I wanted it to be. But I still felt that the edges were too sharp and unrealistic. Photoshop comes with a multitude of filters, and there are more to "plug in" to the program (see "Photoshop filters" in Chapter 2). Unfortunately, there was nothing that would "blur edges" in one easy step. But you can "find edges" and apply Blur or Blur More. I selected the entire image and copied it into a new channel, which essentially converted it into a grayscale image. (By definition, all additional channels in a file after the first four are grayscale channels, which are highly suited to masking operations, as already shown.) Then I applied the filter Find Edges, which turned all the edges white or light gray and everything else black or dark gray (Figure 11). By using the Adjust Levels command, I was able to emphasize the edges of the logo, and then just painted over the extraneous white areas (Figure 12).

Now a special command, Alpha → Selection, selected all the white areas and brought them up in the RGB channel. This meant that the edges of the

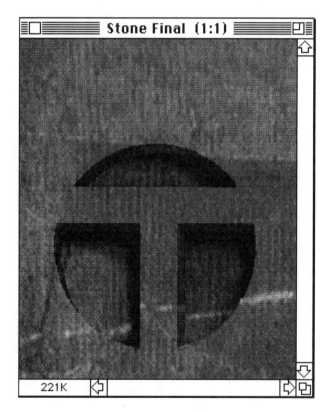

Figure 10. Making the lighting appear more natural. After the second mask was inverted and subtracted, the logo looked better.

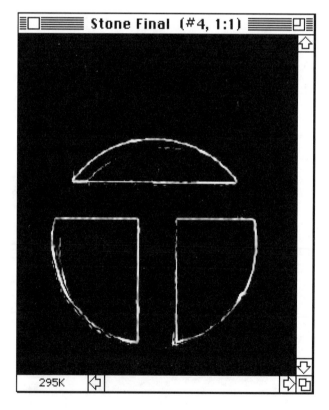

Figure 11. Finding the edges. With all edges turned white (or varying degrees of gray), the input levels could be adjusted to push the darks to black.

logo were now selected and could be blurred independently of the rest of the image. The Blur filter was not enough, but Blur More worked beautifully (Figure 13). I was now satisfied with the image (see page 95).

In retrospect

Since I completed this project, I've figured out a number of different approaches to creating the same effect. I originally formed this image using a set of six or seven separate masks, a clunky "registration bar" I created, and at least four separate versions of the marble with different brightnesses and offsets — much too much fuss, to say the least. The technique that has been described here is much simpler than the original method — the result of several months of experience and hindsight — and produces identical results. It's this sort of learning process that leads to the joy and the challenge of using image-editing software like Photoshop: If you can think of a visual effect, you can probably produce it — your challenge is to figure out *how*.

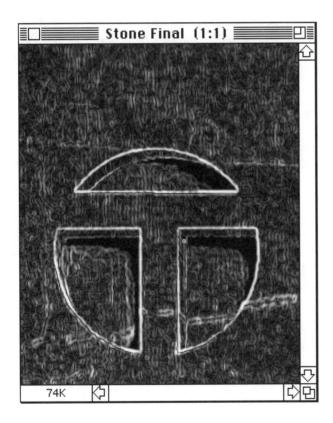

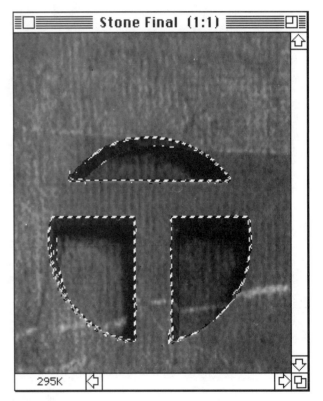

Figure 12. Blackening the rest of the image. Once the darker veins were pushed to black by adjusting levels, the few veins still showing were painted over.

Figure 13. Using Alpha → Selection. This command brought the mask layer up as a selection in the RGB channel — a beautiful way to select the edges of the near-complete logo.

Peter Vanags

"Using the computer for sketching is intrinsically difficult. The indivisible pixel is at once too rough and too smooth — it's constraining in both directions. Sometimes you can't work broadly enough, because you must work with so many pixels at a time; at other times the heartbreak of the jaggies places limitations on your work. I find it critical to sketch and work out ideas on paper before going to the computer, whether or not I eventually scan the sketches as templates. The important part about sketching on paper is creating a mental template that helps me plan out an image before I execute it."

Kimono Girl Neon (top) was taken from a stock photo used for a *Publish* magazine article on color scanners. A Photoshop plug-in (third-party) "impressionist" filter was used to give the image a painting-like appearance. The Find Edges filter was used to generate the "neon" highlights, which were composited with the impressionist version to produce the final image.

Rex (above) is another application of the Photoshop techniques described in this chapter. In this case the effect adds extra character to a name tag designed for a Stanford Design Conference event.

Temple was created with Micro Frontier's Enhance image-retouching software to accompany a review of the software in *Publish* magazine. Islamic script and a human figure were removed from the temple image, and then sailboats were placed in the pond in the foreground, along with the wakes they created. Finally, various parts of the image were colorized with the 8-bit palette replacement and color blending features of Enhance.

The **Skyline series,** reprinted from *The Apple Guide to Publishing, Presentations and Interactive Media,* shows the effects of several kinds of image editing in Photoshop. **Skyline** (left) is the original image as photographed, complete with a flat unappealing sky.

Skyline/Pyramids (below left) is a version with a more dramatically colored sky (especially where it meets the buildings), and a few extra Transamerica buildings.

Skyline/Sunset (below right) was created by darkening the foreground until it became a silhouette, and pasting in the sunset behind.

Skyline/Lightning (bottom) adds a dramatic sky scene behind a color-adjusted foreground.

CHAPTER 7

Video Eyes

Designer

Charles Wyke-Smith spent many years in England doing multi-image presentations (in the old sense, with racks of synchronized slide projectors), which involved audio mixing, programming and slide design. Several years after selling his business, called OnSite, he came to the San Francisco Bay Area to settle. In the fall of 1986 he cofounded Printz, a desktop service bureau providing print, slides and video communication products.

Wyke-Smith has been a pioneering spirit in the use of desktop video in particular. The results that Printz can achieve continue to grow with the increasing sophistication of multimedia.

Project

The project described here was the first TV commercial produced almost entirely on the Mac. Done in the early "8-bit display days," the project was a 30-second trailer for KRON Channel 4 about a TV show called "Addiction to Perfection." In April 1989 the Hal Riney Agency enlisted Printz to simulate a computer graphics machine that would allow a hypothetical user to preview any cosmetic change being contemplated by punching buttons to change various facial features.

Luckily, they wanted a coarse computer look; our 8-bit color PICT files suited their purpose perfectly. At Hal Riney, Doug Patterson was Art Director and Debbie Wiley was Producer.

I used a Mac IIx with 2 MB of RAM, an Apple 8-bit video card, a 13-inch color monitor, a Computer Friends TV Producer Pro genlock/display card and a 13-inch Sony Trinitron NTSC monitor with a Color Freeze video capture piggyback card. I also used an Ikegami video camera and MacroMind Director animation software. (The MacroMind Director artist was Jim Collins.) The TV Producer board, an NTSC conversion device, was used to change the RGB images into a video-compatible signal.

The process

Features from several faces were
assembled in Director's Paint mode. Some
of the faces are shown here. Then we had
to "animate" them by coordinating with the
soundtrack and "tweening" (filling in inter-
mediated views between starting and end-
ing images) for the appropriate number of
frames. After a lot of experimentation, the
various Director files were copied onto
Betacam (a comparatively inexpensive
broadcast-quality video format) at a video
studio and edited together.

Scanning

I scanned one picture for the underlying
face, and then scanned 17 images from
other photographs to capture facial features. The video camera was placed in a
copy stand and the photographs were
placed flat underneath. At the time, 24-bit
flatbed scanners were not common, and
we needed video resolution in any case.

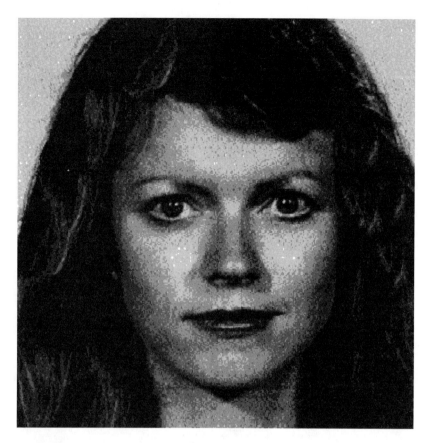

The original underly-
ing face was used as
the basis for applying
changes in the 30-
second trailer for "Ad-
diction to Perfection."

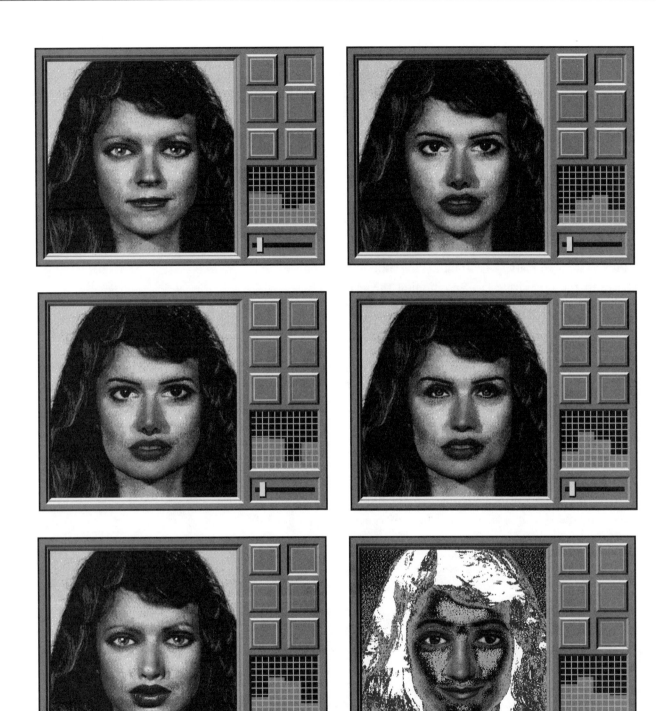

These images show
some of the changes
made to the features
of the underlying face.

For this project the 8-bit "computer" look was what the client wanted. The initial painting part of the project was fairly straight-forward. The photo of the underlying face was opened in Director and used as the background image. To put together the various other faces for the sequence, we needed to cut out features from our original scans. First we used the airbrush, set to white, to put soft edges around a particular feature and to clear a path for the lasso. Then a selection was made with the lasso in the white path left by the airbrush, and the selection area automatically shrank to fit the edges of the feature. The result in each case was a perfectly selected facial feature with a soft edge (Figure 1). ▌ *The feathering option of the lasso in Photoshop serves a similar purpose.*

Next it was simply a matter of cutting the selection to the clipboard and pasting it into the underlying face, positioning the selection and finally touching up white spots by using the eyedropper to pick surrounding colors and the pencil to dot them in (Figure 2).

Animating

Once the altered faces had been assembled, the people at the agency spent a lot of time going over the script and how they wanted things to look. They experimented for three days with such things as the buttons and graph on the computer console.

Each major version of the face was created as its own Director file, for a total of six files (the various quick ones at the end were in one file). To create a file, we placed the changed face in the first scene at the beginning of the score, and then placed it in the same spot later on and "in-betweened." The number of

Figure 1. Isolating features. The airbrush (set to white) and the lasso were used to select each feature with a soft edge from its original face, ready to be copied and pasted onto the new face.

Figure 2. Touching up the combination. The eyedropper was used to pick colors around stray white spots, and then the pencil was used to fill the white dots.

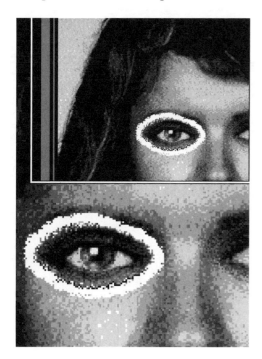

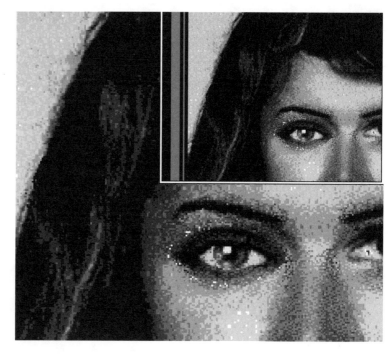

Charles Wyke-Smith

"I first started using the Mac in early '86 when my partner and I founded PRINTZ. Back then, we produced multi-image shows, and it was immediately clear, even from the then top-of-the-line Mac Plus, that computers were about to enter the design and production process at every level. Within two weeks I was using the Mac for scripting, budgeting, creating Linotronic camera-ready art for the optical slide camera, and scanning images into typeset storyboards. Since then, the Mac has actually become the medium itself; linked into a video projection system, it now replaces the banks of projectors we formerly used for big-screen speaker support at business meetings.

"Recently PRINTZ has opened a separate multimedia facility where we're using the Mac for animation, 3D modeling and video graphics, MIDI, digital audio mixing and mastering, scanning and montaging of color images for output as transparencies and color separations. Designing with computers gives us complete control over our productions and lets our clients see meaningful work-in-progress at a much earlier stage."

frames depended on the length of time that face would be on the screen. Each file comprised about 5 seconds' worth of animation.

As the faces changed, the buttons on the side of the computer console seemed to be pushed, as if different features were being tried at the push of a button. Animating the pushbutton action was simply a matter of painting each button in two states, coming out and pushed in (Figure 3). We pasted the pushed-in version in a different place for each facial change.

Finally, to video

The finished files were transcoded to a Betacam recorder via the TV Producer board. The final version of the animation was edited together at the video studio. The type on a black background at the end of the sequence was done on standard video equipment, as was the soundtrack.

In retrospect

Today, I would have attempted to digitize the voice and build it into the Director score. Also, it would have been fantastic to have 24-bit color. I would have scanned with 24-bit color and then mapped down to 8-bit in Director (for speed). Video softens the look of the images, since pixel graininess is reduced when transferring to NTSC.

In addition, there could have been more emphasis on changes occurring as the buttons were pushed. As it was, the effect was almost too subtle — viewers didn't necessarily realize right away that buttons were being pushed throughout the piece. But overall, I was very happy, considering how early it was in the whole Mac-to-video process.

Figure 3. Animating the buttons. One by one, the buttons were depressed. To create this effect, we painted one depressed button and moved it around as needed.

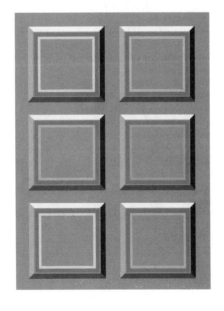

CHAPTER 8

Mythology and Technology

Artist

With a Master's degree in painting and drawing from California State University at Fullerton, Michael Johnson was trained as a traditional painter and illustrator. His aesthetic leanings are toward classical art and mythology.

Johnson turned to computer technology in 1985, shortly after the TARGA board was released for the PC. For eight years he has been Associate Professor of Fine Arts at Cypress College in Orange County, California, where he teaches classes in using the computer for fine arts, presentation slides, illustrations, desktop publishing and broadcast. His work has been exhibited in the United States, Austria and Japan.

Project

One of a series of fine art pieces depicting themes in classical mythology, this project demonstrates some of the timeless themes in the myth of "Leda and the Swan," with a somewhat modern touch.

I used a Zenith 286 with 2 MB of RAM, a 40 MB internal hard drive and a Truevision TARGA 16 graphics board (Truevision Advanced Raster Graphics Adapter), which supports 32,768 colors, real-time image capture at $\frac{1}{60}$ of a second per frame and the ability to overlay computer-generated graphics on top of a live video source. Peripheral to the system were an Electrohome 13-inch RGB TTI RGB analog monitor, a Wise 700 VGA black-and-white monitor, a Summagraphics SummaSketch Plus digitizing tablet, a Microsoft bus mouse; an Epson FX 850 dot matrix printer, an Apple LaserWriter Plus for black-and-white proofs, and a Shinko 335 color thermal printer. For video input I used a Howtek Photomaster analog film scanner for 35mm slides and negatives, a JVC RGB video camera and a Sony CCD video camera.

Bitmap drawing and video scans were done in Truevision TIPS. Development of the composition and high-resolution files was completed in the AT&T RIO system. Finished 32 x 40-inch archival inkjet color prints were made by Jetgraphics in Los Angeles, a service bureau with a large-format Fuji inkjet printer.

**PROJECT
OVERVIEW**

Scanning

Most of the images for "Jupiter Startles Leda" (shown on pages 111 and 119) were captured with the TARGA 16 as composite video images from the Howtek 35mm Photomaster (a slide scanner that outputs a composite video signal). The images were then saved in TIPS .TGA format.

These are several of the component images used to create "Jupiter Startles Leda." The pond is quite an average-looking pond at this point, and the stately swan, with its exact reflection in the water, provided the perfect representation of Cygnus, or Jupiter disguised.

Classical inspiration

Crossing points are those intersections where major but divergent ideas, forces, movements or traditions interface. This project is a story of the interfacing of traditional art and modern graphic technology.

The painting is titled "Jupiter Startles Leda." The impetus for the work came from the mythological encounter of the mortal Leda and the supreme deity, Jupiter, who, after using many masquerades, finally in the disguise of a swan achieves his conquest of Leda.

"Leda and the Swan"

Leda appeared regularly in classical mythology. She was the mother of Pollux and Clytemnestra. The word Leda is of Cretan derivation and is best translated as "woman."

According to the myth, during one of his frequent meanderings, Jupiter, father of the gods and all humankind, observed the beautiful Leda and immediately fell passionately in love with her. His amorous approaches were rebuffed by the faithful wife of Tyndareus. However, Jupiter con-stantly pursued her, changing his disguise after each failed attempt. After one such encounter, Leda fled from her palace, hoping to escape Jupiter by hiding at the edge of the river. The omniscient Jupiter transformed himself into a beautiful swan and gracefully appeared to the object of his passion. Leda did not recognize the latest disguise of Jupiter and, moved by the swan's grace and beauty, reached out to caress the exquisite creature. The seduction of Leda by the god-swan was completed.

These three images, constructed by the same method as "Jupiter Startles Leda," are among the 14-part "Leda and the Swan" series.

One of the paintings in my series based upon the "Leda and the Swan" myth, "Jupiter Startles Leda" shows the moment at which the reflection of the swan-god startles Leda. Leda is not physically present in the picture, only her reflection. Also shown in the reflections upon the water is a palace behind Leda which has just caught fire and is destined to be consumed by the flames; the palace represents the past.

"Jupiter Startles Leda" shows two reflections, or alter egos, taking note of each other, contemplating what it might be like to be together. That the past will be erased, burnt to the ground, is of no concern. This is that frozen moment just before desire and passion become inexorable.

Generating the elements of the composition

I explored preliminary concepts and compositions in my sketch book. For me the sketch book is the best foundation to help define the image material needed to produce the painting. My image material generally consists of 35mm slides, negatives, clip art, magazine advertisements and commercial images, and I start with the background and build forward. For "Jupiter Startles Leda" the background was taken from a 35mm slide of a koi fish pond (Figure 1). Using the TIPS Grab function from the Function Menu, I chose Composite Video (my Howtek 35mm Photomaster uses a composite video signal). The image was then saved in TIPS.TGA file format.

▌ *TIPS allows you to save an image in two different file formats: .TGA, which is a whole screen, and .WIN which is a user-defined partial screen that can be overlaid on top of any other screen. An image saved as a Window (.WIN) can have a surrounding black color, RGB 000, that makes that black area invisible. This is a very handy feature for combining separate images.*

All the photographic elements of the composition had to be generated as Windows with invisible backgrounds before they could be used. The swan, like most video-grab elements (Figure 2), had unwanted foreground and

Figure 1. Developing the background. The fish pond, taken from a 35mm slide that was captured with the Howtek Photomaster and TARGA 16, became the background for "Jupiter Startles Leda."

Figure 2. "Grabbing" the swan. The swan was captured in a similar fashion.

background information. Using the TIPS Function menu, I selected a one-pixel brush, 000 black and a drawing tool that draws a connecting line. Drawing around the part of the image I planned to use, I got very close to the actual shape without going into its form. Once the shape, in this case the swan with its reflection, was completely outlined, forming a ring, I used Fill from the Function menu, set to Boundary Fill. The color of the outline drawn around the form became the boundary of the fill. When the fill color was set to 000 black, the unwanted background and foreground became transparent (Figure 3).

Composition elements used for the house, flames, Leda, lily pads, flowers and koi fish were all slides or video grabs whose backgrounds were removed and saved as Window files on the hard disk for easy retrieval.

Figure 3. Isolating the swan. The swan was isolated by drawing a color line around it. The parts of the image outside the outline were converted to black, rendering them transparent.

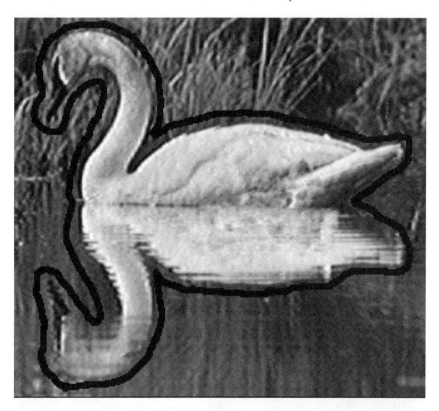

Into RIO

When all the primarily bitmapped work was completed, I left TIPS and moved into RIO, where the composition would be assembled. RIO (an acronym for Resolution-Independent, Object-oriented) has many design features not found in the bitmapped TIPS program. RIO treats all elements on top of the background as objects. All objects can be assigned attributes such as light source, shadows, transparency and placement, which can be modified as needed at any time. A complete description and collection of all elements, background and objects, can be saved as a scene file (.SCN). RIO images are resolution-independent, which means you can print to screen at 512 lines or output to a file or film recorder at 1000, 2000 or 4000 lines of resolution. ∎ *For working with a scene, RIO has a fast-render mode in which objects appear as blocky mosaic representations rather than complete images. This mode is very helpful for composing the design.*

Leda's reflection is the focal point in the composition. To achieve the illusion of a reflection in the water, a Leda file, which had its background removed and was saved as a .WIN file in TIPS, was loaded into RIO. RIO then treated this file as an object that was assigned a transparency attribute only and placed on the background. The image of Leda could now be scaled and moved into place in the fast-render mode, and then the composite was saved as a scene (Figure 4).

Files for the house and flames were brought into RIO from TIPS for placement. The flames were copied a few times on top of the house, and then each flame was individually scaled and assigned a different transparency attribute to achieve the illusion of depth. RIO allows individual objects to be selected and then grouped together as a single object. The flames were now

Figure 4. Introducing Leda. The isolated image of Leda was scaled and moved into position in the pond image.

grouped to the house, and together they became one object, which was moved into place. As objects can be stacked on top of one another by selecting one and bringing it to the front or sending it to the back, Leda was selected and brought in front of the flaming house (Figure 5).

The swan was placed in RIO as two separate images. The image used for the reflection was given attributes for transparency and then was grouped with its counterpart to be scaled and placed into position. Foreground lily pads and koi fish were loaded into RIO and assigned the desired attributes (Figure 6).

Figure 5. Creating the burning house. An individual flame was copied and placed with differing degrees of transparency. Then the flames were grouped with the house, and Leda was brought to the front.

Figure 6. Adding the final elements. The swan, koi fish and lily pads were introduced.

I had been working in the fast-render mode and now it was time to do a final rendering to the screen, which meant each object would be redrawn and displayed in its best form at the current display resolution of 512 x 482 pixels (Figure 7). Final adjustments in scale, placement and transparency attributes were made before the composition was displayed on the screen for a final check. Then it was saved as both .SCN and .TGA full-screen TIPS files.

Finishing the piece

For the final phase of "Jupiter Startles Leda" I loaded the .TGA file created in RIO back into TIPS, where I could use two of TIPS's best special effects features, Duplicate and Blend, to clean up rough edges. Duplicate allowed me to select a part of the composition and duplicate it pixel-by-pixel in a 360-degree radius, using any drawing tool. This was ideal for painting with an existing texture in the image. I selected part of the composition with the desired texture adjacent to a rough edge. Then I drew, duplicating this texture pixel-by-pixel, replacing the unwanted pixels with the selected texture and cleaning up the edge in the process (Figure 8).

Figure 7. Rendering the almost finished piece. The image was rendered and saved in high resolution in RIO before going back to TIPS for final touches.

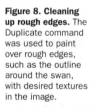

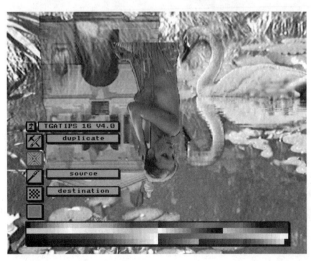

Figure 8. Cleaning up rough edges. The Duplicate command was used to paint over rough edges, such as the outline around the swan, with desired textures in the image.

Figure 9. Blending. Blending was applied most to the background and least to the foreground. This reinforced the illusion of depth and helped to antialias the image.

Finally all the edges of each component got a final polishing with the TIPS blend tool. Blend allows you to set a sharpness level from –2 to +10 (least sharpness to most), and then apply this, using any drawing tool, to your composition. As I drew with the blend tool I made the background recede and further combined the edges of forms with the background, maintaining full control over the amount of antialiasing or blurring that took place (Figure 9). ▮ *Using a low number, 1 or –1 for background work, 4 through 7 for the middle ground and very little blend for the foreground reinforces the illusion of depth within the picture plane.*

The composition was complete and could be brought back into RIO to produce a file independent of the screen resolution (Figure 10). I had 35mm slides made for presentation to clients and galleries. ▮ *The resolution needed for printing on paper or canvas is determined by the machine used to do the printing. For example, Jetgraphics of Los Angeles can print a 32 x 40-inch inkjet print using archival materials.*

In retrospect

The TARGA system gives me the kind of spontaneity and freedom I love, but if there's one thing I miss about traditional painting, it's the tactile quality of the finished piece. The closest I ever get to achieving this is with a printout on canvas. The bumpy, coarse surface really adds something to the piece.

Figure 10. Outputting the image. The finished "Jupiter Startles Leda" image was output in various forms including 35mm slides, inkjet prints and in Amiga's .TGA format which was opened in Photoshop on the Macintosh and saved as a color TIFF for reproduction here.

Michael Johnson

"Tools and materials have been agents of change in the visual arts throughout history. The migration of art through the development and sophistication of tools is not only necessary but imperative. Every blatant turn and subtle shift in history has affected the form, nature and expression of the artist's work, and, in turn, those works have reflected the time that facilitated them.

"And now, Light! I don't mean the illusion of light, but light itself. Light, a new brush in the hands of the artist. We can capture light on film. We can transmit light from the site of the latest collapse of a political system to a satellite high in the cluttered heavens and back down into our living rooms, into our television sets, just in time for 'film at eleven.' Fortunes are made, or lost, through the transmission of light from one terminal to another. Now is the time for artists to adopt the new technologies that will permit them to use the next tools of art, to manipulate light."

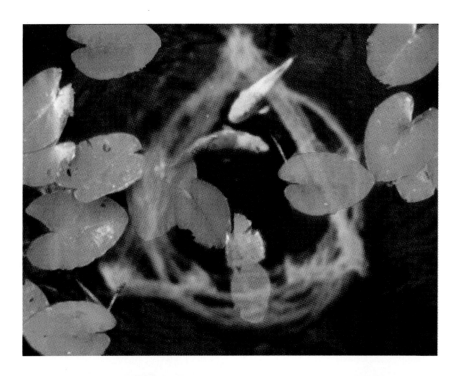

Paramour (top) is the title painting for the "Leda and the Swan" series. The French word means illicit lovers, a title that tells the story of the entire series.

In this painting from the end of the "Leda and the Swan" series (above), Jupiter is seen as a soldier painted on the wall looking at a vase (Leda) painted on the opposite wall. The room is empty except for a chair and flowers, and the floor is flooded with water. The painting is like a stage set — the actors no longer live, but they exist as characters in a myth, waiting to play out the story again.

In **Paradise Lost** (above left), an image in the "Leda and the Swan" series following the mating of Jupiter and Leda, Jupiter is trapped in a ring of fire, trapped by his passion. The remorseful Leda has just crawled onto shore.

In **Escape** (above right), which also follows the mating of Jupiter and Leda, Leda is seen swimming underwater toward the ring of fire left by Jupiter, who has just departed.

Annunciation (left), created in the summer of 1986, was an early digital composed image. It was created using an 8-bit, 256-color Number Nine Graphics board and Xiphias' Sketch 9 painting software.

CHAPTER 9

Through a Looking Glass

Artist

Sharon Steuer is a freelance artist and illustrator living in Bethany, Connecticut. After receiving a B.A. from Hampshire College, she went on to pursue postgraduate studies in painting and drawing at the Portland School of Art, the Yale School of Fine Arts and the Vermont Studio School, and then studied computer graphics at the New York Institute of Technology.

For the past six years she has produced computer fine art and illustration for companies including Apple Computer, Letraset USA, SuperMac, Electronic Arts, Ashton-Tate, Silicon Beach, *MACazine*, *Publish*, American Express and Travelers Insurance. She developed the official training course for Letraset's ColorStudio and has written articles and reviews on computer graphics for *Computer Currents*, *Macworld*, *The Weigand Report* and *Step-By-Step Electronic Design*. She is also a private consultant and instructor. Her drawings, paintings and computer art have been exhibited nationally.

Project

This image is the result of explorations with Letraset's ColorStudio 1.1 and was reproduced in the official ColorStudio training seminar manual.

Three stock photos were scanned into ColorStudio using the Nikon LS 3500 slide scanner and assembled, scaled, rotated and manipulated using ColorStudio masking and retouching features. Color corrections were applied to the image both globally and selectively. After the image was proofed on a film recorder, the monitor was recalibrated to match the slide

and a final color correction was applied. The completed file occupied 797K compressed with StuffIt, 1467K uncompressed.

This image was produced using a Macintosh II with a 32-bit 4 MB NuVista color board, 8 MB of RAM, a partitioned Jasmine 140 MB hard disk drive, a Sony 13-inch color monitor and a GTCO Macintizer digitizing tablet. It was printed to an Agfa Matrix PostScript film recorder for 35mm slide output and also color separated through ColorStudio's Crosfield DeskLink for print reproduction.

**PROJECT
OVERVIEW**

Letraset's training seminar

To develop the official training seminar for
ColorStudio, I decided to create a new image using ColorStudio's high-powered
masking, assembly, retouching and painting features. My intention was to create a
personal image from stock elements, as
in some kinds of collage. The Mac and
ColorStudio allowed me to be spontane-
ous and work seamlessly between the idi-
oms of photography and paint, without
having to worry about the difficulties associated with glue and airbrush. In short, I
was able to build the image intuitively, in a
way that would be impossible with traditional materials.

Dreaming up an image

Placing two stock photos together was
merely the inspiration for what would eventually become an art piece characteristic
of my personal imagery. As is true to my
method of working in traditional media
(oils and chalks), I had no preconceptions
about how this image would develop. The
cone of the teddy bear's dunce cap suggested a party hat, and it inspired me to
create a birthday party scene.

"Birthday Party with Kitty" was created from
these two images. In the stock photo of the kitten, its furriness could present some difficulties,
but at least the kitten was light and the background was dark. The pronounced contrast
would make it easier to separate the subject
from its ground. Elements of the little girl's setting could be changed to indicate another context — namely, a birthday party.

ColorStudio provides tools for painting, masking and color correction. In "Birthday Party with Kitty," for example, I used the masking function to put clouds inside a painted window frame and then used the paint tools again to divide the window into panes. Correcting the color made the image appear softer and more pastel.

n search of an inspiration for an image to be used as part of Letraset's ColorStudio training seminar, I pored through a folder full of stock photos that had been scanned by Letraset. Each of the photos was saved as both 75 dpi and 150 dpi PICT files so that I could work with the lower-resolution files (which are half as large in terms of the computer memory they occupy, and therefore twice as fast to work with). Later, I could selectively drop in the higher-resolution images for final output. After days of thinking about these photos, I thought of placing an image of a white kitten behind the girl in a photo titled "Overwhelmed Little Girl" as a first step in building an image called "Birthday Party with Kitty" (see page 124).

Using masks

I took the scan of the "Overwhelmed Little Girl," cropped it, and repositioned her to make room for the kitten on the left. Since the repositioning had considerably increased the area above her head, I had to extend the pinkish background color to cover the black space. I used the lasso to copy an area of the background, selected the black areas and pasted the background color into the new selection area. ▌ *In ColorStudio the copied area is automatically resized to fit into the new selection shape, just as in ImageStudio.*

To place the kitten behind the girl, I had to create a mask that protected the girl and her chair. In ColorStudio the simplest metaphor for understanding the masking layer is that black = transparent, white = opaque, with grays in between. Since the mask layer is 8-bit full grayscale, images can be masked with any degree of transparency from fully opaque (white) to fully transparent (black). For my current needs, I had only to place a white mask over the little girl and her chair and let the mask remain transparent (black) around her.

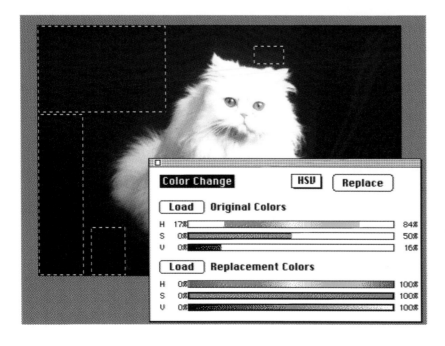

Figure 1. Creating a mask. The image of the kitten presented a relatively direct path to creating a complete mask. The first step in making the near-black background a solid black was selecting as many nonblack areas as possible and then pushing them to black.

The Mask layer in a PICT image begins as completely black (transparent), so I selected the areas I wanted to protect with white. In the Image layer I used the polygon and lasso tools to trace (and thus select) from the left edge of the chair inward. ▮ *Holding down the Shift key adds to the previous selection; the Shift and Option combination subtracts from the selection.*

Then I chose to copy the selection to the Mask layer as Solid White (from the Mask menu). Though the Image layer remained unchanged, the Mask layer was now prepared for me to place the kitten into the image. (I didn't protect the desk surface behind the chair or its contents, as I had decided to remove them from the image.)

Preparing the kitten was a little more difficult. I wanted to select the kitten but not the black background — and since I didn't want to trace every piece of fur by hand, I had to create a cookie-cutter type mask for the kitten itself.

I first selected the entire image (Select All) and copied it to the Mask layer as Solid White (opaque). To isolate the figure from the background I decided to make the almost-black background entirely black, knowing that black can be made transparent. Using the selection rectangle and holding down the Shift key, I selected as many of the background grays as I could identify. Opening the Color Change dialog box, I then Loaded the selected grays as the Source colors (Figure 1). To make the Destination Color exactly black, I manually adjusted all of the sliders to 0 percent (0 percent of all colors equals 100 percent black). I then selected the entire image and clicked the Replace button; the ColorStudio program searched the image for any of the colors listed in the Source range and substituted 100 percent black for those colors. The result was a solid black replacement of the entire background (Figure 2).

Figure 2. Going to black. None of the selected colors were present in the kitten itself, so the Color Change dialog box could be used to convert a broad range of dark colors to black.

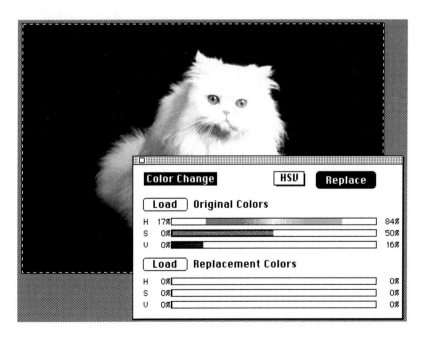

Using the Auto Selector tool set to "Match on Exact Color," I clicked on the new black background. This selected the entire black background, which I then copied to the Mask layer as Solid Black. Because the background perfectly outlined the kitten, the Mask layer now had a solid white kitten surrounded by a transparent black background (Figure 3). This mask would now work as a stencil to protect the kitten as I pasted it into the other picture.

Returning to the Image layer, I drew a selection rectangle around the kitten (background included) and copied it. I saved this version of the kitten, in case I needed it later, and closed the file. Returning to my "Overwhelmed Little Girl," I pasted in the kitten, which remained selected, floating on top.

Figure 3. Making a perfect stencil. The solid white part of the mask would protect the kitten.

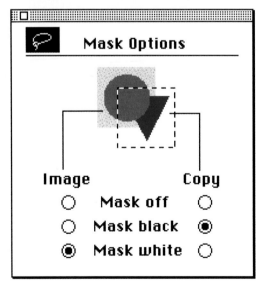

Figure 4. Layering the images. The mask for each image can be assigned a different task. In this case, the kitten image was assigned to the white part of the Mask layer and the background was assigned to the black part of the Mask layer.

Opening my Mask Options window, I adjusted the transparency so that the Image mask was white and the Copy mask was black (Figure 4). This floated the kitten, without the black background, behind the little girl.

The kitten was too big and at the wrong angle, so I opened the Dynamic Effects window (Figure 5). After clicking the Try button, I scaled the kitten by about 60 percent and manually rotated it into position. Clicking End, I then nestled the kitten into position and pasted it down by double-clicking the selection rectangle.

Retouching tools

Various portions of the image needed retouching at this point. The edges of the kitten needed to be blended into the background, portions of the desk had to be removed, the edges between the kitten and the chair needed smoothing, and I needed to create shadows and light.

ColorStudio provides many tools for painting and retouching. Among the tools I used were the paintbrush and airbrush, used with a variety of options, pen shapes and transparency levels. The Paint With Part Of Image option (which allowed me to repeat an image, or part of an image, elsewhere) and the Start Of Stroke option (which allowed me to drag one area of color over another) are both powerful touch-up tools. With the waterdrop tool, the smudge tool and various filters I was able to blur hard edges to smooth the transitions of color.

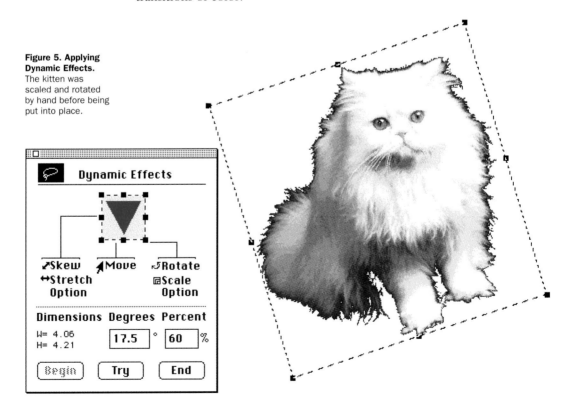

Figure 5. Applying Dynamic Effects.
The kitten was scaled and rotated by hand before being put into place.

I changed the "A: Apple" card to "C: Cat" by pasting and reducing another copy of the kitten and using the curve of the small "a" to shape a big and little "C" (Figure 6). Using a variety of paint tools, I made the teddy bear's dunce cap and the little girl's sun bonnet into party hats.

I lived with the image for a few days, trying many ways to balance the right side of the picture. Eventually I decided to place a stock photo of a beautiful blue sky with fluffy clouds in a window behind the girl.

To create the window, I painted the sills and shadows using the airbrush tool; holding down the Shift key allowed me to draw straight lines. I used the smudge and waterdrop tools, also using the Shift key and a high transparency level to create smooth transitions for the window sills. To protect the girl as I was creating the window sills, I painted her in a White, opaque mask. For

Figure 6. Painting details. Parts of the image were changed by hand using ColorStudio's paint tools.

every tool I was using, I checked the Mask White option, which allowed paint to be applied to everything except where the mask was white. ■ *In addition to seeing the separate, grayscale view of the Mask layer, you can also view it as a film of a specified color on the Image layer. The mask can be thought of as a monochrome overlay on the image.*

When the outer sills were pretty much in place, I put a transparent mask in the window pane area, preparing it to receive the clouds. When I opened the cloud file, I chose Read Into Private Scrap so that instead of opening a new image window, I would load the clouds into virtual memory, ready to paste into my Birthday Party scene (Figure 7). Clicking the Preview button allowed me to crop out the black area around the clouds. ■ *ColorStudio uses virtual memory (hard disk space) to store clipboard, special effects and undo files; this allows you to work with files much larger than the RAM of your computer would otherwise allow.*

Returning to the Birthday Party, I pasted the clouds on top of the image and then adjusted the Mask Options to drop the clouds properly into the masked windowpane area. I smoothed the transitions again between figure and ground. Using the Start Of Stroke paint option, I dragged out vertical and horizontal windowpane dividers, working and reworking them until I was satisfied with the illusion of a light source (Figure 8).

Figure 7. Using Private Scrap. You can use your hard disk as a special kind of clipboard by selecting Read Into Private Scrap when you open a file.

Figure 8. Adding clouds and windowpanes. Pasting and adjusting mask options neatly cropped the clouds within the window. Vertical and horizontal windowpane dividers were added using the Start Of Stroke paint option.

At this point I decided to insert the higher-resolution (150 dpi) version of the girl, her chair, toys and teddy into the Birthday Party scene. I first increased the resolution of the Birthday Party image to 150 dpi (at this point, the image looked the same but was smaller in dimension). I then opened the 150 dpi version of the "Overwhelmed Little Girl," selected the areas that contained the increased resolution that I wanted and copied the areas to the Private Scrap. In the Birthday Party scene, I protected the areas of the sky, the birthday hats, new shadows and transitions to surrounding areas so that when I pasted the girl she would appear only in the regions that I had selected. I then pasted the 150 dpi little girl into the Birthday Party scene, placing her into position and adjusting the Mask Options so that the new areas were visible only in the regions that were unprotected by a mask. ▌ *By being selective in the use of high-resolution scans, you can work more quickly and easily, less encumbered by large, memory-hogging images.*

I had overworked a couple of areas of the kitten; in trying to create shadowed areas, I ended up losing the texture of the fur. To reintroduce the fur texture into those areas without losing the value changes I had made, I created a value mask of the overworked areas by selecting them and choosing Copy To Mask: Value. I then rechecked and touched up the opaque mask protecting the edge of the chair so that the new overlay would remain behind the girl.

I reopened my copy of the kitten with the black background and recopied the kitten into the Private Scrap. After pasting the new kitten into the Birthday Party, I resized and rerotated him to match the previous kitten. I then adjusted the Mask Options so that the new kitten was lying transparently over the previous one, effectively merging the value of one kitten with the texture of the other one (Figure 9).

Finally, color correction

As "Birthday Party with Kitty" was becoming one of my fantasy images, I wanted to soften the harshness of some of the color contrasts to unify the colors of the image. By using the auto selection tool set to Match On: Close Hues I was able to select only the clouds. Command-clicking in one of the selected areas isolated the floating selections so that I could apply Color Correction to the selections only.

Opening the Color Correction window, I both lightened and increased the cyan components of the clouds and adjusted the color of the little girl's face. I then selected the entire image and adjusted its color components to achieve a softer, more unified color range (Figure 10).

After printing to a film recorder, I determined that the little girl was too "hot" (there was too much red). ▌ *ColorStudio allows you to calibrate your monitor when opening the program, by holding down the Option key and double-clicking. A printed card comes with the program to help you match the colors on-screen to the same colors printed.*

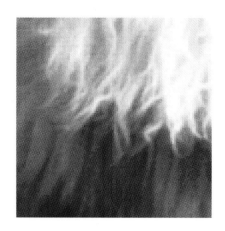

Figure 9. Regaining lost texture. Transparently overlaying the original kitten on top of the overworked one restored some of the texture that had been lost.

Figure 10. Correct-ing color. Color Cor-rection was applied to selected parts of the image to achieve a softer color range.

Figure 11. Saving the color correction. You can save your color correction set-tings to disk and ap-ply them to the image later, or to an-other image.

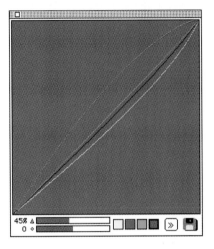

By renaming my Birthday file as the calibration file, I was able to use it to calibrate the monitor to match the slide. I then went into the file and, selecting the girl, created a Color Correction that compensated for the red. I saved these Color Correction settings to disk (Figure 11). Because I knew that the final image would be separated and printed to paper, I did not fully trust a "slide-reliant" calibration of my monitor. Using the normal calibration file supplied with ColorStudio, I recalibrated my monitor to match the printed color-matching card. With my monitor now calibrated for print, I reopened "Birthday Party with Kitty" and retrieved the saved Color Correction to see how it looked. It turned out to be close, and after some minor adjustments I applied the final Color Corrections. I was now reasonably sure my file would work in both printed and slide form.

For the *ColorStudio Training Seminar Manual*, the final piece was sepa-rated through ColorStudio's Crosfield Link. Other versions of "Birthday Party with Kitty," in 8-bit grayscale and black and white, were also used for the manual. Sometime in the near future I plan to produce birthday cards and a limited edition of fine art prints of the image.

In retrospect

I feel that the finished piece, "Birthday Party with Kitty," though constructed of impersonal photos, was transformed into an image that bears a striking resemblance to my more traditional works in oils. The effect of combining photos with paint, however, could never have been achieved without the development of the computer as an artist's tool.

Sharon Steuer

"I have always viewed the computer as a new, exciting printmaking tool. I can combine photographic and painted images seamlessly, create endless variations of what would normally be a 'finished' piece, then eventually print limited editions of final images. Unfortunately, 'output' is still the weakest link for the computer as an artists' tool. With current technology, my output method of choice is to print final images as transparent Cibachromes lit from behind in light box frames. Someday, however, I plan to collect my favorite images on disk and develop a way to print them more traditionally as fine art limited editions."

Margi with Sunset was painted with a GTCO Macintizer tablet and Color-Studio. After the portrait was completed, Color-Studio's Mask feature was used to drop the Nikon-scanned sunset into place behind Margi's head, and some fine adjustments were made to the lighting and shadows of the figure.

Maya is the first in a series of works that constitutes a collaboration with Photographer Norma Holt. It was begun by applying color to a scan of one of Holt's black-and-white photos, and then simplified by eliminating some elements. A Mayan warrior was painted on another page, and painting and masking features were used to combine it with the tinted version of the photo.

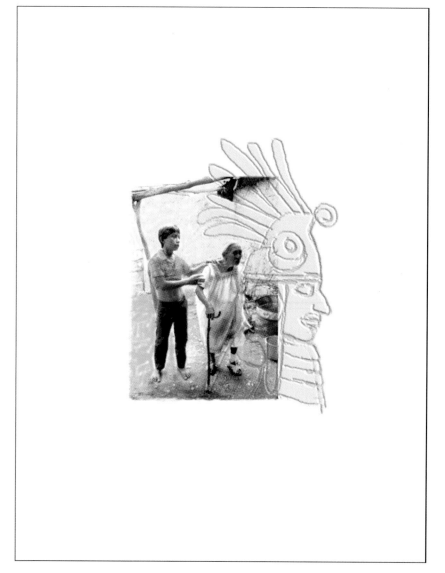

The mythical **Kolokolo Bird** began as an Apple Scan of a snapshot of a toucan. The scan was very dark and non-descript, a blotchy black-and-white image — perfect as a jumping-off point. The image was completely repainted in ColorStudio. A scanned sunset sky was dropped in behind the bird. Its colors were changed from oranges to pinks and combined with a textured pattern for a soft surreal look.

Elephants Marching started with a quick sketch made with an electronic tablet in ImageStudio. The sketch was imported into ColorStudio, where scaling and masking features were used to multiply and alter the elephants into a marching herd. The combination of painterly marks and photographic backdrop created a diorama effect. This image and the "Kolokolo Bird" are part of a series of images created for a multimedia "animatics" presentation of Rudyard Kipling's *The Elephant's Child* commissioned by IMT Inc. of Scottsdale, Arizona.

C H A P T E R   1 0

Still Video Vision

Artist

David Brunn has been in the forefront of digital photography since 1985, when he first started working with the Mac. With over 17 years of training and experience in traditional photographic techniques, Brunn has been able to bring a full body of knowledge to the new technology. Experienced with large-format photography, platinum prints, mixing his own chemistry and making his own glass plates, he considers himself to be of the Weston school, and yet has been sold on the Mac ever since he first saw MacVision and MacPaint.

Brunn has heartily embraced the "video Polaroid," in particular the Canon Xapshot still video camera. Image resolution is low compared to a photographic slide, but for newspapers much of the resolution of a slide is lost in any case. The benefits of the still video camera in terms of convenience and cost are considerable.

Project

I decided to develop a project that would put still video technology to good use in a visual and interactive database about airplanes called "A Walkaround Series on Famous Airplanes." I used the Xapshot to create 360-degree walkarounds of more than 50 planes of historical interest. For display, a Macintosh monitor set in a museum wall would be equipped with a touch screen, allowing anyone to access a complete visual library interactively and perhaps more thoroughly than would be possible otherwise. The Smithsonian Institution has expressed an interest in the project.

Part of the project involved creating the opening screen of each plane by modifying a shot of a hand-painted model in Photoshop so it seemed to be in flight. I captured these images and placed them into SuperCard via ColorStudio. Each of these three programs has its own most useful features.

In addition to the Xapshot, I used a Computer Friends 32-bit video capture board, called the ColorSnap 32, to grab the still video images, and a Mac II with an Apple 8-bit video card and 13-inch RGB monitor.

A two-part project

I needed a frontispiece for each aircraft in the series. For the title art for the P-40 WarHawk, for example, I used a model plane, a real sky and the Canon Xapshot camera.

After completing the frontispiece, I created the rest of the plane's photo series. Using several kinds of software, I removed visual distractions from real-life scenes. All the skills I had learned over the years in the darkroom I could now transfer to the Macintosh — without the fumes and burned hands.

Scanning

Since Computer Friends had made scanning drivers for Photoshop and ColorStudio, frame grabbing from the Xapshot was simply a matter of pulling down the appropriate command in the File menu of each program. Images can be grabbed in grayscale almost in real time.

The still video shot of the P-40 model was captured with the ColorSnap board within Photoshop.

This still video shot of the sky was used as the backdrop for the model, which would look like it was flying through the skies after the composite image was modified in Photoshop.

The Xapshot image of a real P-40 was captured within ColorStudio. This image would be touched up and used as part of the chapter about this plane.

T here were two parts to creating this interactive SuperCard stack about airplanes. Each made use of different source material and different manipulation programs. For the first part I used Photoshop to combine a still video shot of a hand-painted model of each plane with a shot of clouds and sky, and then I added certain artistic touches to bring the scene to life. The finished "in-flight" image was then used in the opening screen for that plane's "chapter" in the stack. For the rest of the project I used ColorStudio to retouch my walkaround shots of the real planes before bringing them into SuperCard.

Photoshop and the Flying Tiger

The P-40, or Flying Tiger, was one of the most colorful and memorable fighter planes. For the purposes of this SuperCard stack, I wanted to introduce the plane in its natural element, with a sense of drama and realism.

Over the years I've collected a number of hand-painted airplane models from Italy, the Philippines and elsewhere. For the SuperCard screen I photographed my model of the P-40 on its pedestal, at an angle and with the macro lens option of the Xapshot (which is better for close-ups). The result, brought directly into Photoshop via the ColorSnap board, was quite acceptable. Unfortunately the right wing and one propeller blade got lost in the shadows (see page 140), but this could be fixed later.

I had also captured a number of sky shots with the Xapshot. I selected a section of one of these and resized it to fill the screen (Figure 1). This would serve as the background for the plane. ∎ *Photoshop's ability to resize images is excellent, but sizing up eventually degrades the image unacceptably. Use your eye to judge, and avoid sizing up too much.*

The next task was to isolate the P-40 from its current background, add a wing to it and clean it up before pasting it into the sky file. I cropped out the background by lassoing the plane and copying it, double-clicking the eraser and pasting it down (Figure 2). (I could have used the Crop command under

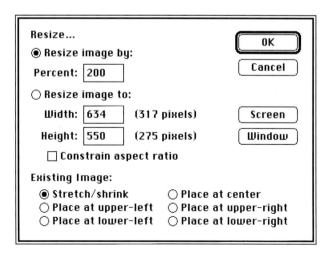

Figure 1. Resizing the sky. The selection of sky was resized to the dimensions of the screen. Photoshop interpolates pixels to create the larger size.

Photoshop's Edit menu to perform the same trick.) Then I used the eraser to clean up the edges.

To add a propeller blade, I selected an existing one, Option-dragged it to copy it, and finally rotated and skewed it to make it look right (Figure 3). I then increased brightness and contrast slightly (Figure 4). Color balance can be adjusted in a similar fashion as brightness and contrast. In this case I adjusted the midtones "up" and the shadows "down" (Figure 5). ▌ *These adjustments can also be made on a small selected area rather than the whole image.*

Figure 2. Cropping the plane. A quick lasso around the plane helped to isolate it from its background.

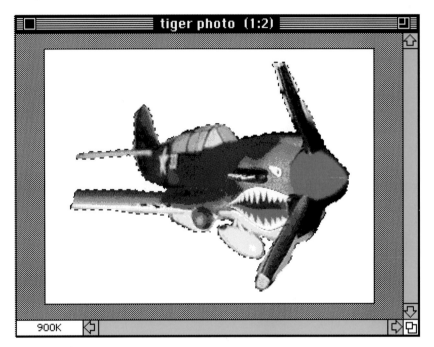

Figure 3. Adding a propeller blade. After the eraser tool was used to clean up the edges, copying, rotating and skewing an existing blade produced the new one.

After the smudge (fingertip) tool was used for smoothing some jagged edges, the plane was almost ready to be dropped into the sky. The feathering option of the lasso would come in handy for performing this task. ∎ *The feathering option allows you to select an area and adjust it in much the same way as you would burn and dodge or use various filters in the darkroom. The feathering keeps the blending effect smooth and gradual around the edges.*

First I double-clicked the lasso tool and set feathering to 5 (Figure 6). Then, using the magic wand, I selected the white space around the plane with a click. Choosing Inverse under Select caused the plane itself to be selected (Figure 7).

Now I could copy the plane and paste it into the sky. ∎ *Option-Paste brings up a dialog box with a number of Paste options, including degrees of transparency.*

Because of the feathering, for the most part the edges of the plane blended smoothly with the background (Figure 8). However, I did need to smooth some edges with the smudge tool.

Artistic touches

If a plane is to look like it's flying, it helps to bring out or add certain effects that might be visible in reality, such as contrails caused by moisture in the air. I concluded that these and other effects would help bring this hand-painted model to life.

First, I needed to add the wing that originally got lost in the shadows. To do this I took small sections of the other wing, Option-dragged them over to the right with feathering, and distorted them slightly to get them into the right shape (Figure 9).

After smoothing the edges of the wing into the sky, I continued the smoothing around the canopy and engine. As in sculpture, it can be a good idea to keep working all the way around the piece so one area doesn't get overworked.

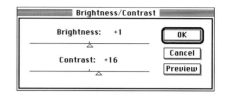

Figure 4. Adjusting contrast and brightness. Contrast and brightness were increased slightly by moving the sliders to the right of their center points.

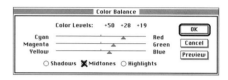
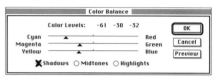

Figure 5. Adjusting color balance. The sliders affect the image on-screen as you watch. Shadows, midtones and highlights can be manipulated separately from each other.

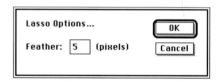

Figure 6. Feathering a selection. For most instances of pasting one image into another, 5 pixels is a good setting for feathering.

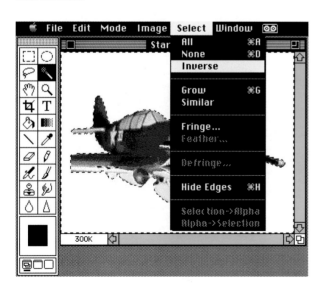

Figure 7. Selecting the plane. Since the background was one color, the magic wand could select that easily. The inverse of that selection was the plane.

Around the prop I decided to add some contrails to help create a sense of wind and turbulence effects. I have many photos of these effects. With these images in mind, I began to smear clouds over the prop blades to create the sense of moisture whipping around the prop as it cuts through the air (Figure 10).

There were no clouds in the immediate area of the wings so I selected small sections of the nearest clouds and Option-dragged them over. Then I simply smeared these around the leading and trailing edges of the wings. In addition, I wanted to see sparks and hot vapors flying out of the engine. I copied and Option-Pasted a section of clouds to bring up the Paste controls dialog box. Then I adjusted the floating selection to create a translucent effect and bring up the brighter pixel points, creating the effect of sparks and hot vapors (Figure 11).

Figure 8. Putting the plane in the sky. The feathering helped the plane fit "seamlessly" into the background when it was put in place.

Figure 9. Creating the second wing. Option-dragging selections of the existing wing furnished the raw material for constructing the missing wing.

Figures 10. Creating contrails and motion blur. Smearing white clouds in the direction of motion across the propeller helped to create the illusion of motion.

A few small tasks remained: touching up the right wing, adding a white highlight to the prop nose with the airbrush and smudging it in a circular motion, selecting some colors on the plane with the eye dropper and airbrushing them back to create a sense of blur, and touching up the mouth and eye. At this point I pulled back to view the whole picture and then moved in again to finish smoothing out some areas and blending some rough edges. Then I pulled back once more, added some touches to the exhaust, belly and wing tip and typed my copyright notice in the corner. This completed my work in Photoshop (Figure 12).

I added the title and put the image in a window in SuperCard, reduced to fit (Figure 13). Now I had an image that could be used both as an illustration and as the starting piece for a walkaround in SuperCard.

ColorStudio and the walkaround

The remainder of this project was a straightforward exercise in retouching with ColorStudio. ■ *With the kind of flexibility and power given to us by*

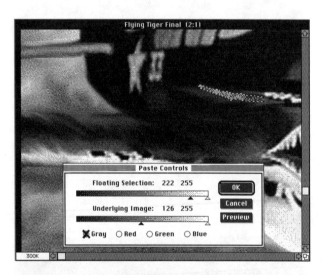

Figure 11. Creating engine exhaust with Paste controls. The interplay between floating selection and underlying image was adjusted so the piece of cloud looked like exhaust from the engine.

Figure 12. The final piece. After some final touch-ups, the base image was complete, ready to be converted into a SuperCard screen or used in its own right for hard-copy output.

programs like ColorStudio and Photoshop, it becomes very easy to get carried away with painterly effects. As in the case of traditional retouching, subtlety and restraint are the key words. Especially with these new tools, obvious retouching can be regrettably easy to achieve. To use these tools and still maintain some degree of realism, added colors should be based on colors already present in the image.

The walkaround part of the stack maintains a very factual, documentary style. One of the walkaround shots of the P-40 has a distracting row of people and a white line crossing over the plane. (Two common problems with photographing air shows are the presence of crowds and the rope that's used to keep people from venturing too close to the planes.) To remove these distractions without altering the realistic look of the scene, I carefully removed the white rope by Option-dragging small sections of adjoining background over sections of the rope. Done properly, this technique usually doesn't require a lot of blending or smudging (Figure 14).

In ColorStudio you can view several different magnifications of a file at the same time. You can keep a 100 percent view open and work in a 200 or 400 percent view; any edit will be reflected in the original view. A 400 percent view was very helpful for analyzing the pixelation of a given area, such as the area occupied by the people and bordered by the tail of the plane and the horizon line (Figure 15). At this magnification the individual pixels became distinct colors and it became easier to pull the image apart. A 200 percent view made it easier to see mid-range areas that could be blended.

First I blended the treeline down, covering the upper parts of most of the people (Figure 16). With the smudge tool I could blend some pixels to get a base and then smear it. This was done carefully, as the human eye is quite

Figure 13. Putting the image in Super-Card. The image was sized down slightly for SuperCard, and a title was added.

sensitive to changes in palette and pattern. ❚ *A smear with the finger tool sometimes doesn't provide the full range of colors that are picked up by a still video camera, so a careful mixing and modulation of pixels is critical to good retouching. A good procedure is to touch in and smear to get a base and then use a selection to drag and copy. If you need to modulate colors a little, double-click on the current color and ColorStudio's convenient Color Matcher will appear with the current color selected.*

Next I did a little color correction to make the background slightly darker and the foreground richer. This is very similar to balancing color lines and adjusting the gamma of photos in the darkroom when making color prints. The area where the people stood was now dark enough to allow a more subtle blending.

The final result looked natural and quite acceptable (Figure 17). Additional walkaround shots were retouched in the same way to complete the "chapter" on the P-40.

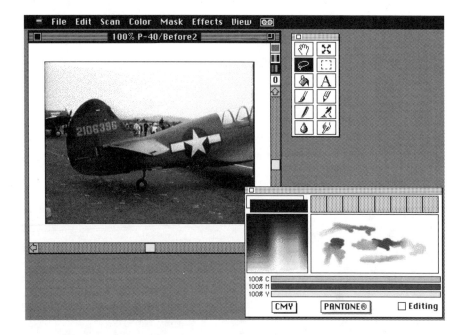

Figure 14. Eliminating the rope. Option-dragging adjoining sections of background in ColorStudio neatly covered the rope.

Figures 15. Using interactive magnifications. Views at 400 percent and 200 percent were very helpful for performing subtle retouching. The editing performed in one view was automatically updated in all other views as well.

In retrospect

I can show the frontispiece for the P-40 in full scale to clients and say to them, "This image of an airplane could be a building [or whatever a client's product is], and this is the photo magic that I can create for you." Clients, I have found, like proven techniques. "Don't learn on my time," they say. So I produce my own projects that will test the newest software and hardware. These projects are about subjects that interest me and that I'll be able to market after I've finished testing. So the image I created of the P-40 is an art piece for my own use, but clients' eyes get big when they see the model used to create the image. Then they understand what I can do with this new medium.

Figure 16. Extending the tree-line. The tops of the people were covered by extending the elements on the horizon.

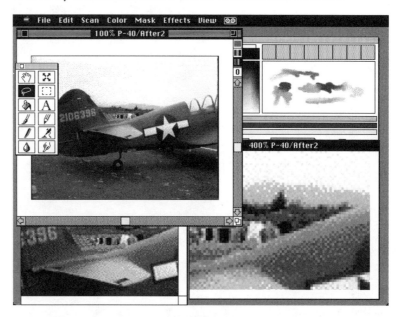

Figure 17. Comparing the result with the original. The final result (right) compared favorably with the original image (left).

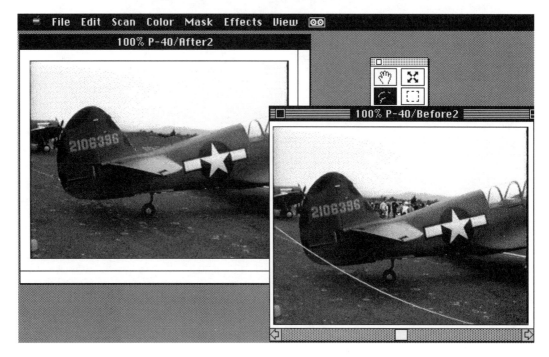

PORTFOLIO

David Brunn

"I've always said the Mac is the great Cuisinart, giving us the ability to regrind other images. The ability to combine images and create visual illusions is for me one of the most attractive features of digital photography. My camera is focused inward.

"Each photographer should strive to add to or help expand photography's power. This is done with the strength of the photographer's images and with the tools available at the time. My tools are still film cameras, still video cameras and the Macintosh computer. Through the merging of the photographic images with the capabilities of the computer, I have opened a window on my imagination. Places that existed in mankind's past are raw material for me. They bring up feelings of lost knowledge and forgotten wisdom.

"I always tell people that I'm not a computer artist. I just happen to look into my camera bag and see a Mac (and now a Xapshot as well). I still own and love my 8 x 10 view camera, but I don't think someone who runs around with an Insta-matic is a wimp. New art always arises out of a need, and the point is to use any tool that can help you fill that need."

Sky/Owl (top) was built in Photoshop — using an owl and a barren landscape — both still video shots captured with the Xapshot and the ColorSnap board.

Sky/Rock (above) was composed in Photoshop with captured still video images. The textures of the rock are suitably apparent. The relatively low resolution gives the image a soft look overall.

Coastal/Celtic, celebrating the supremacy of nature, is an ImageStudio synthesis of still video images captured with the ColorSnap board.

Temple/Owl was composed in Digital Darkroom. The image makes use of the same owl image used in Sky/Owl, but in a different still video–captured setting.

CHAPTER 11

Magazine-Quality Specs

Designer

Phil Inje Chang first put desktop technology to use in 1985 while publishing a literary arts magazine called *Shades of Gray*, a magazine he had produced traditionally since 1980. He began to develop his technical understanding of digitized imaging while performing technical support for Microtek scanners in 1986, and in 1987 he copublished a magazine emphasizing PostScript called *showpage*. He has since applied desktop publishing in the areas of advertising, graphic design and print production while writing about the technology for *MacUser, MacWeek, Computer Currents, Personal Publishing, Verbum* and other publications. Chang's thorough knowledge of traditional methods and his academic background in semiotics (the study of meaning) provide a foundation for his current work in high-tech marketing and on *Shades of Gray*, a journal of aesthetics and technology.

Project

This project was an experiment performed on behalf of a client with extremely tight time constraints. The client was Graphisoft, a European software developer beginning to market a high-end architectural CAD product in the United States called ArchiCAD. The object was to create and produce a four-color, full-page ad for *Builder* magazine, a thick, glossy publication for professionals in the construction industry. Since only about one week remained before the deadline and since recent advances in desktop technology made four-color production feasible, we decided to use desktop publishing.

Hardware included a Macintosh IIcx with 8 MB RAM and an internal Quantum 80 MB hard drive, an Apple 13-inch color monitor with a SuperMac 24-bit display card and Graphics Accelerator and an external 140 MB hard disk with a built-in 44 MB removable cartridge drive. The scanner used was the Array AS-1 multiformat, high-resolution scanner. Scanning was done on a PC AT equipped with Truevision's Vista board. The image was saved in .TGA format and sent over TOPS to a Mac, where it was opened in Adobe Photoshop for color correction, image editing and four-color separation and in QuarkXPress for page layout and printing. Kent De Sena and Array's Director of Marketing, Bo Varga, provided support.

The campaign

Part of the beauty of desktop methods is the ability to streamline many design decisions into one overall design/production task when necessary. In this case, an entire campaign had to be devised and implemented in one week.

Since there was no time to get a photo shoot approved, I decided on a straightforward approach to the ArchiCAD ad with emphasis on a catchy headline. I chose Garamond condensed for the headline. (The font was condensed slightly more than Apple's official corporate version.) After some rough comps were presented, the client chose "Spec this out," which plays on the program's ability to help builders design their own buildings and list the materials necessary for construction.

What remained was the task of converting a 4 x 5-inch transparency into usable form. There were a few problems with the photograph. First, the image showed a warehouse — a commercial building — but the primary audience of *Builder* magazine consisted of residential builders. Also, the product box showed a noticeable banding in color, a flaw in the production of the box. However, both problems could be corrected in Photoshop.

The original scan of the 4 x 5-inch transparency had two problems that were later corrected in Photoshop: First, the photo was of a commercial building (while the magazine's primary audience was residential builders). Second, there was a flaw in the box itself — visible color banding that had occurred during production.

Scanning

The decision to "go desktop" depended partly on the existence of Array, a multiformat scanner capable of 6000 x 6000 lines of resolution. In this case, an additional challenge was introduced because the image had to be enlarged at least twice. A simple calculation revealed the necessary resolution (see "Calculation of resolution" on page 155).

Unfortunately, this presented a difficult choice. At 2000 lines, the image when enlarged and screened at 150 lines per inch for printing would come close to one and a half samples per halftone cell. Two samples per cell is the figure usually recommended. However, the scanner could only scan at 2000 or 4000 lines, and 4000 would yield a file approximately 40 MB in size. Although a removable Syquest cartridge could hold such an image, I predicted considerable trouble down the road with manipulating such a file and saving it in the Photoshop five-file format required by QuarkXPress, so I settled on the 2000-line scan.

The scanning was performed at Array's corporate office by their technician, assisted by me. A quick prescan helped us position the original correctly and judge the effect of various compensation factors on the richness of red, green or blue and the shadow detail. The prescan seemed undersaturated, so we boosted the red significantly and started the half-hour scan.

Photoshop's five-file format produces a 1-bit PICT file for placement in Quark-XPress. At print time, QuarkXPress looks for the four separation files and prints at the proper screen frequencies and angles.

knew of a number of risks involved in producing the ArchCAD ad with desktop means. Foremost among them was the resolution at the enlarged full-page bleed size, but I was convinced that the Array scanner could support the necessary resolution. Another was the potential for difficulty in PostScript screens. Interference patterns, called *moirés*, sometimes result from the interaction of screen frequencies and angles in the four-color separations produced by the imagesetter. I knew that Photoshop and Quark-XPress employed Adobe's recommended frequencies and angles when printing PostScript separations, which eased my worries about this risk, and I had seen fairly nice samples from DPI, a color service bureau in San Francisco that uses the Agfa Compugraphic imagesetters.

Scanning at 2000 lines, we produced a base file in RGB Photoshop format that came to 7940K. The five-file encapsulated PostScript (EPS) version for QuarkXPress took up about 13 MB. Even for this relatively small file, I needed substantial working space on my hard disk. So my guess proved correct: Even at a scanning resolution of 2000 lines, I would be pushing the limits of my system.

Color correction

The first scan done at Array Technologies was slightly crooked and weak on red. Photoshop could easily rotate a large image like this in 90-degree increments, but the rotation needed to adjust the angle of this image proved impossible with the 23 MB of free space I had available on my hard disk. So a second scan was performed, this time with better prescan adjustments.

In this second scan, the main image looked undersaturated, or washed-out, especially in the red part of the spectrum. Instead of adjusting overall saturation, I went into the Color Balance dialog box in Photoshop's Adjust pop-up menu and started playing with the levels. Immediate response shows how moving the sliders in the dialog box affects the image. Shadows, midtones and highlights could be adjusted independently (Figure 1).

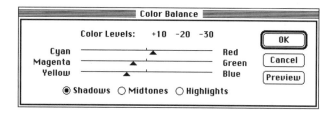

Figure 1. Adjusting color balance. The red, green and blue on-screen colors and the cyan, magenta and yellow that would print were adjusted through Photoshop's Color Balance dialog box. Red and magenta were increased in the midtones and shadows, and cyan was brought out in the highlights.

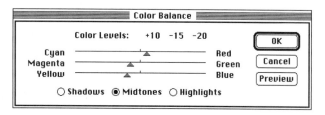

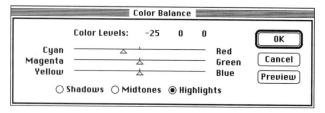

Calculation of resolution

The calculation of necessary resolution is a fairly simple matter. As a general rule, oversample if possible. That is, within the limits of your data handling powers, use as much scanning resolution as possible. So the question really becomes one of: What is the minimum scanning resolution?

If we call the dots of the scanner samples, then make sure there are two samples per halftone cell in the final printed, screened piece. In other words, consider the linescreen or frequency of halftone dots (not total printer dots) and double that figure, then multiply by the width or height of the final printed image. This will give you the total number of samples needed for that one dimension. For high-resolution devices, resolution is often referred to in total lines (usually in K or thousands), rather than dots per inch. In the case of the scan in this project, the image had to be 9 inches wide, and printed at 150 linescreen. So I needed 300 x 9 = 2700 or 2.7K lines of resolution. Since I settled for a 2K scan, I was not quite achieving two samples per halftone cell.

In the case of flatbed scanners that are typically measured in dpi, take the total samples for one dimension, divide by the actual dimension of the original, and the result is the necessary scanning resolution in dpi. In the example above, I would have needed 675 dpi, since my original was 4 inches wide.

Retouching

Besides needing color correction, the main image had two inherent problems. The first was the image that appeared on the screen of the computer in the picture. It was decidedly blurry and bluish, but in addition the content was inappropriate. I decided to re-create the screen image by using ArchiCAD and PICT Viewer on a Mac to show a residential project, and then captured the screen as a color PICT file using the Capture program. I pasted the resulting color PICT into the Scrapbook and brought it into Photoshop (Figure 2).

▎ *To help Photoshop create a new window at the right size for the Scrapbook image, copy the image from the Scrapbook first, and then select New in Photoshop.*

After resizing the new screen image, I selected, copied and pasted it into the main image. I had to undo and resize it several times to get it to fit within the monitor. By the time it did fit, the image had become a little broken up, but it was still much sharper than the original screen image.

The second problem was the uneven coloration of the product box. After selecting a rectangular section of an unbounded area, I Option-dragged the selection over the flawed area and used the finger tool to blend the edges of the patch and smooth it in place (Figure 3).

This concluded the editing of the image. Now I had to convert to CMYK and save an EPS file for QuarkXPress.

Conversion

So far, I had been working in Photoshop's RGB mode, the raw format for most scans. RGB includes four channels, one for each of the three colors and

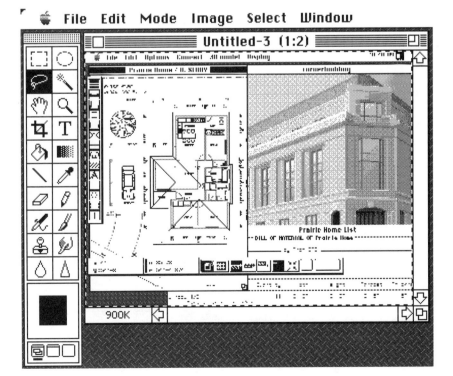

Figure 2. Creating a new screen image. A new screen image was set up, captured and brought into Photoshop.

one for the three together. Editing typically occurs in the combined RGB channel, where the image can be seen "as is."

For conversion into the four process colors needed to produce separations for printing, I selected CMYK mode. After the conversion, the file was larger and could no longer be viewed in full color. CMYK mode has one channel for each of the process colors but none for the combined image. Selecting EPS format when saving from CMYK mode revealed the 5-file option required by QuarkXPress (Figure 4). Clicking the Desktop Color Separation box caused Photoshop to save a file for each channel as well as a PICT preview file to be imported into QuarkXPress. I clicked the Binary Encoding button because QuarkXPress accepts the binary format for PostScript, which takes up less space than the ASCII coding.

I had problems saving in EPS format because of an apparent lack of disk space. After clearing up to 80 MB on the external drive and moving Photoshop to that drive, there still wasn't enough room. Then Adobe tech support helped me discover that the Array software saved images at a huge size. When I checked the size preview of the file (by Option-clicking on the file size in the lower left corner of the image), I discovered that it was about 300 inches wide in reality (and sampled at some ridiculously low number like three samples per inch)! The PICT file based on this size would be correspondingly huge — hence my problem with saving in EPS. After changing the width to 9 inches in Page Setup, causing the sampling rate to come up to 170 or so samples per inch (Figure 5), and saving the file in Photoshop format with the new setting, I was able to save in EPS format without a hitch. I'm not certain exactly how much disk space Photoshop needed to handle the resized file, but the number was probably about 30 or 40 MB.

Figure 3. Touching up the box. Option-dragging selections of surrounding color and a little smudging corrected the problem of banding on the product box.

Into QuarkXPress and out

The last step in producing the ad involved importing the PICT file into the QuarkXPress document along with the type. In QuarkXPress I was able to

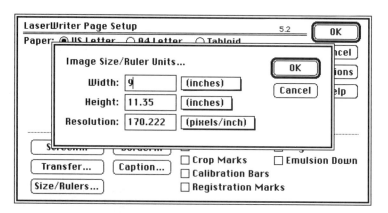

Figure 4. Saving in 5-file EPS format. The 5-file format, otherwise known as DCS, appears as an option when saving in EPS from CMYK mode.

Figure 5. Adjusting the image size. The Size/Rulers button in Page Setup was used to adjust the actual dimensions of the image. (This adjustment doesn't change the amount of data.)

Phil Inje Chang

"I have always felt that the Macintosh and PostScript are innovative in an anachronistic sense — they employ state-of-the-art technology for the purpose of re-creating a piece of paper. Yet it is this fact that is most responsible for their overwhelming success. Traditional forms of communication must evolve slowly, not change radically. If technology is to serve any end, let it be our increased understanding."

resize the image and place it appropriately (Figure 6). The bleed size for *Builder* magazine is 8¼ x 11⅛ inches, so the final width of the image came to 8¼ inches. A laser print showing the positioning of type relative to the picture as well as some last-minute text changes was faxed to the client, and it was agreed that I should move the top of the monitor away from the headline somewhat. Then it was simply a matter of copying the QuarkXPress file to the Syquest cartridge with the five image files on it and taking that to the service bureau. Their 24-hour service allowed me to see a traditional Matchprint proof based on the separated film the next day.

There seemed to be some moiré toward the back of the table, although we knew that this was partly because the Matchprint was hand-registered; it wouldn't be a problem in the final printing. But the screen image looked good and the overall image was attractive.

In retrospect

Although this project was a challenging test of desktop capabilities, in a sense it involved normal benchmarks. In the world of professional photography, 4 x 5-inch transparencies are commonplace. Producing a full-page bleed from a 4 x 5-inch photo would not worry most color shops. Intermediate resolutions from the Array scanner would be very useful for magazine production. The 2000-line resolution scan produced an image that wasn't as sharp as it could have been. A resolution of 4000 lines would have guaranteed the sharpness, but I might have needed an extraordinary amount of free hard disk space to manipulate and save the image in the appropriate format.

Figure 6. Placing the image. The image was finally placed, positioned and sized in QuarkXPress.

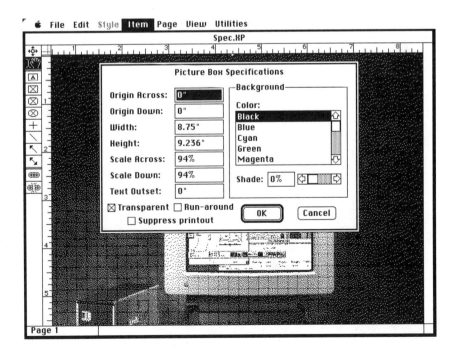

Gallery

Paragon of Distraction (below and a detail at right) began as a composite of two photos, one that provided the background sky (scanned on a Nikon LS3500) and another of the artist's arm (scanned on an HP ScanJet Plus). The photos were combined and enhanced in Photoshop. The water was a duplicated sky with some color correction and filtration. A wire-frame ring was created in StrataVision 3d and assigned a metal attribute with a gold base color. The Photoshop elements were imported into StrataVision 3d to improve the reflections, and then the image was returned to Photoshop for final retouching. The image was output as a 35mm slide by an LFR Plus film recorder.

Greg Vander Houwen is Operations Manager at Heath/Zenith in Seattle. Before becoming involved in microcomputer sales and management, he was trained in broadcast and cable video production. Currently he conducts cutting-edge experimentation with graphics hardware and software for his own recreation and in support of the Veritechnology sales staff.

The **Metamasque** series combines manipulated scanned images with hand-drawn imagery. It was created on a Mac II using a 256-color flatbed scanner to scan the mask images, which were brought into PixelPaint.

Although known primarily for her freehand mouse painting, **Dominique de Bardonneche-Berglund** has recently begun to incorporate scanned imagery into her paintings. Now living in Geneva, Switzerland, de Bardonneche-Berglund is a French painter who's work has been exhibited throughout Europe.

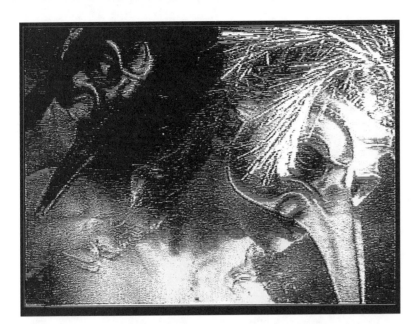

The original still video photo for **Bird Women** (left) was taken with Canon's 701 still video camera and played back on the Canon RV-301 player. To convert the shots to digital form on the Mac II, he used a Truevision frame-grabber board. The image was converted into black-and-white with PhotoMac and then brought into ImageStudio, where the image was sharpened and slight modifications were made. Finally, it was hand-tinted in PhotoMac.

   Photographer **Alan Brown** is owner of Photonics Graphics in Cincinnati, Ohio, a computer illustration company specializing in digital imaging and photo manipulation.

Uwa'yi Akta' (below) means "hand-eye" in Cherokee. The hand-eye/rattlesnake image by **Lind Babcock** was scanned in black-and-white on an Apple Scanner, the contrast was increased, and the image was saved in 32-bit PICT format as large as memory would allow, since it would be output to film recorder for enlargement to 16 x 20-inch prints. In Photoshop the image was lightly tinted, and the Noise and Find Edges filters were applied. The features were digitized with a still video camera, modified in a separate document and pasted into the image. The stair-step motifs in the background were drawn in Aldus FreeHand, Option-copied and pasted into the scrapbook, and then pasted from the scrapbook into a separate Photoshop file for softening, coloring, and finally pasting into the master image. (See page 181 for more work by and information about Babcock.)

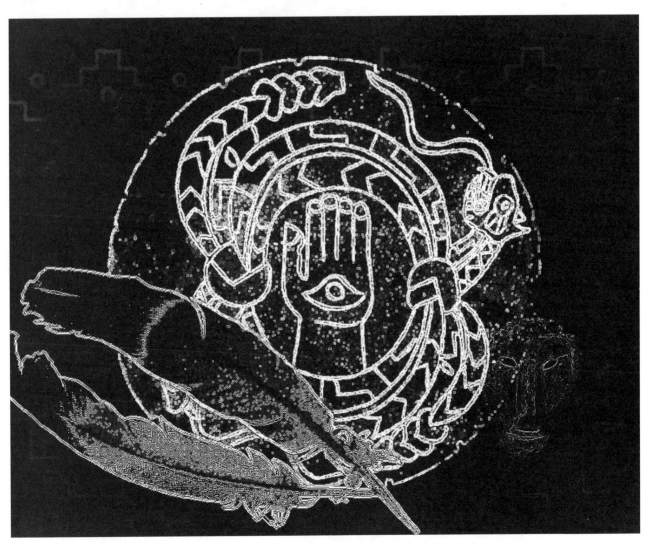

Get 1 (top) and **New New Tupper Title**
(bottom) are "redigitized illustrations,"
created by scanning hand drawings,
printing them out and then scanning
them again as many times as necessary to achieve the desired pixellized effect, and finally manipulating them further in MacPaint.

Paul Rutkovsky, of Tallahassee,
Florida, is the editor/publisher of the
satiric tabloid paper *Get Doo Daaa
Florida* and is an associate professor in
the Art Department at Florida State
University. As a concept artist,
Rutkovsky has created large-scale in-
stallations in outdoor environments and
has exhibited computer-assisted artwork since 1985.

Boy (left) is part of an animated sequence composed of variations on this image. The sequence was developed with a Canon 701 still video camera. PhotoMac, Studio/8 and Modern Artist were used to manipulate and color the images on a Mac II.

Birth (below) was composed in PhotoMac from two separate still video shots, a backlit shell and a baby in its mother's arms.

Jacqueline Domin is a practicing video computer artist in Honeoye Falls, New York, where she produces short films using the Macintosh computer and Canon live video equipment.

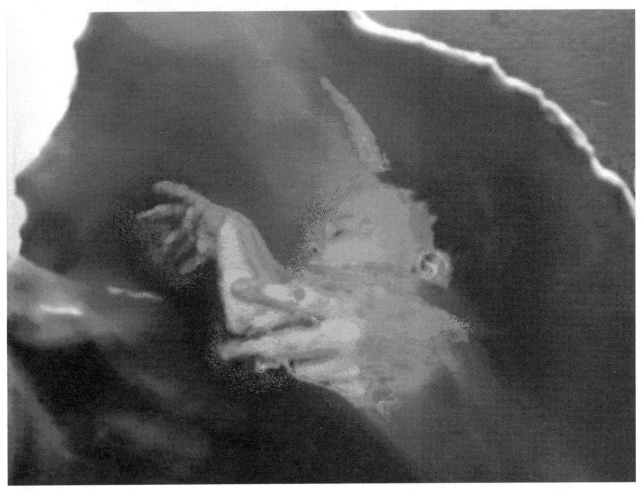

These prints, **Slash and Burn** (top right), **High Speed Chase** (spread), **Forest House** (bottom left) and **Road House** (bottom right), were created as composites of many conventional photographs taken at different times and places, scanned with Thunderscan and blended with Digital Darkroom. The 6 x 20-inch panorama format lends itself to a narrative image that tends to be read from left to right.

David Herrold is an associate professor and chairperson of the Art Department of DePauw University in Greencastle, Indiana.

To create **Double Women No. 2,** a photo was scanned at 300 dpi with a Dest PC Scan Plus, saved as a TIFF in Image-Studio, where the grayscale was modified, and then cut and pasted into PixelPaint for composing and painting.

David S. Brown, Jr. is a fine artist who also uses the computer to create corporate slide presentations, computer animation sequences, print graphics and "electronic paintings."

George Observed Contemplating Truth and Weighing Recent Congressional Testimony was created with SuperPaint as a composite of various images, including George Washington's face from a dollar bill, scanned with a video camera and the MacVision digitizing system.

Lawrence Kaplan lives in SoHo, in New York City, where he is a painter and a graphic designer. He uses the Macintosh to create storyboards for slide shows and videos for corporate communications for such companies as AT&T, Coca Cola, *The New York Times* and Citibank.

Sculpture 2 (above) and **Sculpture** (left) were created in Adobe Photoshop from scans of 3 x 5-inch photographs taken with Ilford HP1 film. The finger/smudge tool was used to blend the busts into the bases, which are a series of graduated-fill rectangles. The sharpen tool and filter were used to sharpen the hair and eyes. In order to have greater control over the contrast and brightness of the images, the Levels dialog box was used to lower the midtones.

   David Palermo of Carlsbad, California is an Apple Systems Engineer who works late into the night on his artistic endeavors while listening to electronic music which inspires his work.

After the Romance (right) began on the Macintosh with two photographs of violins that were scanned and saved as TIFF files. The images were then posterized in Adobe Photoshop, where each of the four displayed gray values was saved as a separate EPS file. These files were then reassembled into a single PostScript file on the NeXT. A PostScript procedure was used to create the blend, and the central curved line was positioned between the posterized layers.

Symphony, Opus 1 (below) also makes use of scanned images that were saved in EPS format. Several of the scanned images were manipulated with Icon on the NeXT. The texture in the piece is a PostScript font, BitFont, written by the artist.

John F. Sherman teaches graphic design and is the Director of Design in the Department of Art, Art History and Design at the University of Notre Dame. He works with both Macintosh IIci and NeXT computers exploring the creative uses of the PostScript page description language and hypermedia.

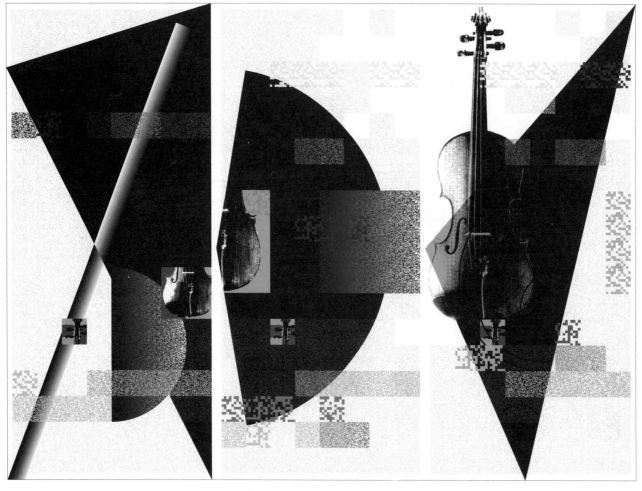

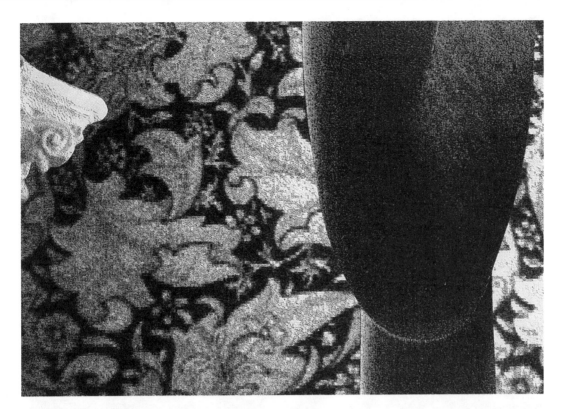

Cultural Drift is part of **Sandra Filippucci's** Stone Age Series of "digital monotypes," one-of-a-kind computer paintings that combine printed sheets from a color inkjet printer with hand assembly and painting. The series was created on the Amiga with a DigiView video digitizer system to scan a photo of the moon's surface and "map" the texture onto various forms in the paintings.

Filippucci lives and works in New York City, and has exhibited her large-format works at many galleries.

Philosophy and Modern Semantics was developed with DigiPaint and DigiView on the Amiga. Inkjet prints were hand-rendered and assembled as a collage. The final digital monotype was used as a book cover for Paragon Books.

Freedom of Expression, for Image Banks' *Europe 1992* catalog, is also a digital monotype created with PhotonPaint, DigiPaint and PhotoLab on the Amiga, output on an inkjet printer, hand-rendered and assembled.

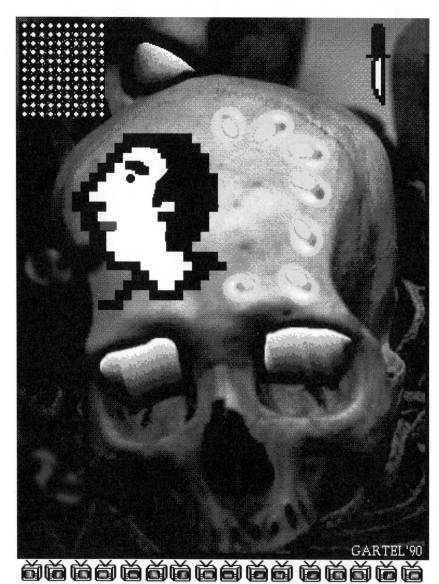

Big Hand from the West (above) is an image painted with DeluxePaint III on the Amiga and further manipulated with the Paik-Abe Synthesizer from a photo scanned with a Jones Frame Buffer using Buff Palette software. The final image, reproduced here from a 35mm slide, is a 20 x 24-inch Cibachrome print.

Skull2 Final (right) is a Macintosh-created image from a photograph taken in New York's Natural History Museum with a Nikon camera and Ektachrome EPP film. The photo was scanned on a Nikon LS-3500 slide scanner. The scanned image was manipulated in Pixel-Paint, and the final image was enhanced in ColorStudio.

Night Life (bottom), from a photograph taken with a Nikon camera and Fuji film for part of a series on tourists in New York, was scanned with Amiga Live software and manipulated using the Fairlight CVI. The work was then rescanned with the Barneyscan slide scanner and further altered in PixelPaint Professional.

New York City native **Laurence Gartel** has been working with computers as fine art tools since 1975, and has exhibited his digital paintings all over the world. He works with mainframe systems and Amiga, IBM/Targa and Macintosh systems.

GARTEL '90

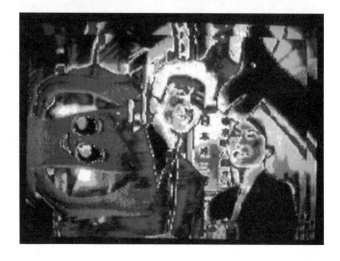

In **Golden Sphinx,** a Canon Xapshot was used to photograph a 35mm slide image that was projected onto a wall. The still video image was captured with a ColorSnap 32 board and taken into Letraset's ColorStudio for manipulation.

Hawk Watcher (below) is composed from two separate images; an original still video frame of the hawk and a 35mm slide projected onto a wall and photographed with the Xapshot. The ColorSnap 32 board was used to capture both images, which were combined and manipulated in Adobe Photoshop.

David Brunn is a photographer and illustrator working extensively with digitized imagery and multimedia. He lives and works in Lake Oswego, Oregon.

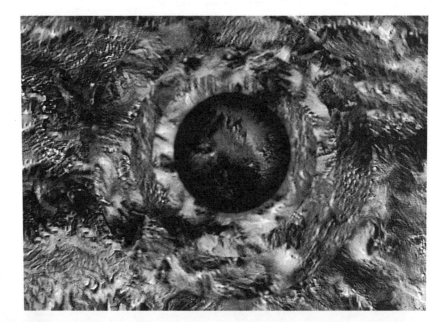

Using Lumena paint tools to convert video scans of various found images, original artwork and photographs, **David Sherwin** of Berkeley, California produces unusual and beautiful works from source material that is heavily image-processed, often to the point of "losing" the original image. Sherwin scans images in low resolution, which he uses as a guide when later converting the file to a higher resolution. He then works on the pieces directly in the higher resolution, varying from 1000 to 8000 dpi. The pieces on these two pages, **Untitled** (right), **The Battle** (below) and **Untitled** (opposite) as well as the images on page 180 were developed in this manner.

The **Verbum t-shirt** image (right) was created for a 2-color promotional t-shirt for the magazine. The base photo from *Index Stock/Black Box* was scanned as a TIFF file. The type was done in Illustrator and imported into Photoshop, as was the custom-designed Swivel 3D Professional robot.

For **Verbum 8-balls** (below), textures of marble were first scanned into Photoshop where they were combined with the color strips and typography. These final 150 x 150 pixel square images were then projected onto spheres in Swivel 3D Professional, rendered as large as possible, and then brought back to Photoshop for adding the soft-edged shadows.

Jack Davis is an artist/designer/editor for *Verbum* magazine, who tries to keep his sanity by punctuating his overindulgences in front of his Mac with time spent surfing in Indonesia, lecturing in Japan and watching *Buckaroo Banzai* in his home in La Jolla, California. (More of Davis's artwork appears on pages 175–177.)

Bow Down (below) is a close-up of an image created for a cassette cover and "J" card. The original image is from an old Doré woodcut Bible illustration. This was scanned at 300 dpi and then brought into Photoshop. The Facet filter was applied to soften the pixelated look, and then the airbrush was used to add the rainbow glows on the figures. The background radial fill was created in Studio/32 and then brought back into Photoshop where the Add Noise filter was applied.

Water (bottom) is a "comp" for a logo for a swimming pool chemical company. First a stock photo of a pool was scanned into Photoshop, where its contrast and brightness were changed to produce the graduated look. The type was set at 200 points in Photoshop and the Minimum filter was applied to it to create a bolder version. This was then filled with the light-to-dark water image. Another copy of the original type was then placed on top and filled with a dark-to-light version of the water. The Zig-Zag filter was applied to the entire image to produce the waterdrop ripple.

Touch (right) started with a black-and-white photo of a neck massage. It was manipulated in Studio/8 with transparent paint and the blend effect. (The art on these two pages is by **Jack Davis.** See pages 174–175 for more work by Davis.)

The images in **Blendo** were created as part of a self-portrait series and then altered and combined in Photoshop for a *Verbum* magazine cover. The 3D models were created in Swivel 3D Professional with custom reflection and texture maps scanned and manipulated in Photoshop. Each photo and 3D image was edited separately, and then they were combined in Photoshop, where the shadows and glows were added.

PreBorn is part of a self-portrait series. This 8-bit, 1024 x 768 montage was created entirely in Studio/8 from images scanned on a Sharp JX450 color scanner.

The original linework for **Stef's Candle** (left) was created by designer Stephanie Whalen as a promotional piece for Professional Printing Services of San Diego. It was imported into Photoshop and filled with eight scanned images used as textures. Although 4-color separations for this image took only 20 minutes to output on an L-300 with RIP 30, a version of the image filled with Adobe patterns in Illustrator 88 (not shown) took 10 hours to produce CMYK separations on the same imagesetting system.

The **Commodities Globe** (below) was part of an image created for a video cassette cover for a financial consulting firm. The gridwork of photos was "spherized" with a Photoshop filter. The highlights and shadow were added afterwards.

The first step in producing **Hercules** was creating a granite texture for the background by painting with a random texture brush and then embossing it for a three-dimensional effect. A color photograph was scanned, converted to monochrome and then to a high-contrast black-and-white image and combined with the background for a "live" template. In Oasis, the Artist Brush was set to 70 percent transparency with stipple density and brush wetness set to medium. Custom pastel colors were mixed on the palette, and the natural look of the pastel brush strokes was enhanced with the pressure-sensitive Wacom digitizer tablet. The image was saved as a 512 x 480 pixel .TGA file and is reproduced here from a 4 x 5-inch transparency

Woman in Chair (below) was developed from scans of a pencil sketch and a canvas (for a textured background), and brought into Oasis. Working on the Macintosh with a Wacom tablet, the artist set the Artist Brush to a very low density to gradually build up the tones.

Chelsea Sammel, a professional illustrator, transferred her artistry to the computer only recently. Previously she had been frustrated with the medium's lack of the look and feel of traditional tools, which has been lessened with the advent of pressure-sensitive tablets.

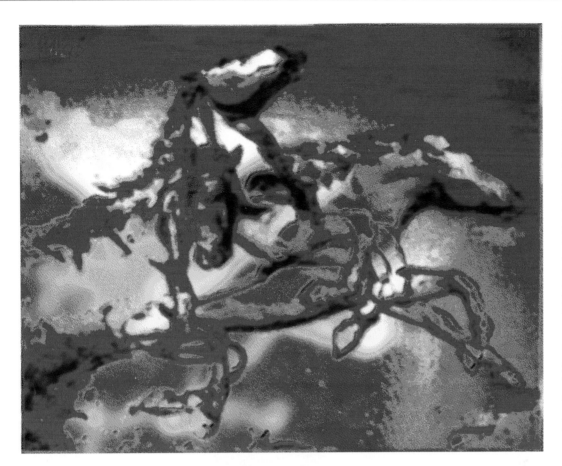

Fire and Horses was assembled using the Incrustation feature in Olduvai VideoPaint 1.0 together with Adobe Photoshop's masking and colorization functions and Gaussian Blur and Facet filters. Of the three images used to compose this piece, only the horses are immediately obvious; the other two, buried in the background, are a wide-angle photograph of rainforest trees and an enlarged electron micrograph of human red blood cells.

Township (below), composed of newspaper photos from South Africa, was assembled with VideoPaint 1.0. The grayscale source images were opened in Adobe Photoshop, colorized with the Hue/Saturation adjustment function and exported as 8-bit PICT images. The photo of the police line was lightly sprayed over the building in the foreground with Masking and Incrustation.

Bennett's Bed and Breakfast (left) makes use of Adobe Photoshop's Noise, Facet, Wave and Gaussian Blur filters along with its colorization function. The elements were treated separately and then combined with Photoshop's Blend function and VideoPaint's Incrustation feature. Source images included various newspaper photos and William Bennett's own official portrait from the Office of Drug Control Policy press kit.

Michael Swartzbeck began his art career as a cartoonist, first gaining notice with his "comix" in the alternative press of the late '70s and early to mid '80s. Discovering the Macintosh in early 1985, he began producing abstract photomontage art using ThunderScan and MacPaint. He has since expanded his media base to include GraphicWorks and Studio/1, Studio/8, VideoPaint and Adobe Photoshop. See Chapter 3 for more art by Swartzbeck.

Landscape is a video scan of a black-and-white print of a southwest landscape that was converted to a 1000 dpi file in the Lumena paint program. Original textures were brought in and used as paintbrushes to re-create portions of the image such as the sky. The final image was output as a digital slide on a Samurai film recorder.

Scarab (below) was produced from scans of source material that artist **David Sherwin** manipulated with the Lumena paint program. (See pages 172–173 for additional pieces by Sherwin.)

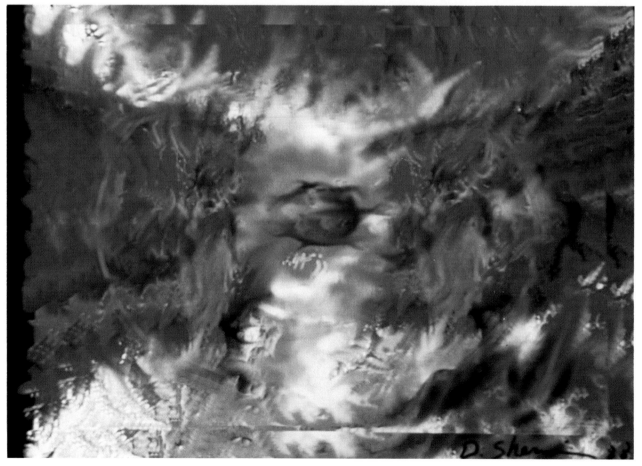

January 12, 1933 was assembled and colored in Photoshop from old photographs digitized on an Apple Scanner. Ada appears as a young child, from a wallet-sized photo taken in 1888; as a teenager, from a graduation portrait and as an older woman. The vivid reds give this image almost a sense of violence that is contradicted by the sleeping figure at the bottom, Ada's estranged husband. The central figure looks as though she is made of flames. This look was achieved by applying the Find Edges filter and then colorizing the image bright red. The sky background was made fiery through the use of the Arbitrary Color Map function. The postmark was scanned from a letter mailed to the woman, edited in a separate file and copied and pasted; with each paste, the postmark was scaled, rotated, tinted and its opacity was controlled before the pasted image was deselected.

Lind Babcock is an assistant professor of art and design at Purdue University, where she teaches visual communications design. Her computer artwork has been exhibited at the State of Illinois Building Gallery, Milliken University, Northern Indiana Arts Association, Syracuse University, Purdue University, Illinois Wesleyan University and the art show for the seventh annual symposium on Small Computers in the Arts in Philadelphia. She has also written about computer art for *Step-By-Step Electronic Design, Computer Graphics World* and *Designer*. (See page 161 for more work by Babcock.)

Family Plot (below) and **Family Plot 2** (below left), showing the dynamics of male and female family relationships, are the first two images in a series of 12 family portraits by **Linda Ewing.** The artist used Targa 16 Truevision TIPS RIO on an IBM clone and Ron Scott's QFX (software for special effects) to combine and manipulate various photographs of family members, sometimes into the way she would have liked the relationships to have been.

Ewing, a Los Angeles county resident with a BA in art from the University of Redlands, works on a Macintosh at her home to develop newsletters and brochures for her clients. She has recently returned to school and is studying under Michael Johnson (see Chapter 8) at Cerritos College.

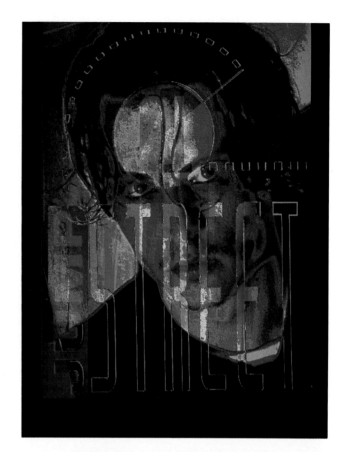

Jump Street (right) was created as a self-promotional piece and *Workbook* ad for artist **Bruce Brownwood.** The logotype was designed in Illustrator on a Mac IIx. Black-and-white output of the logo and a photograph of one of the *21 Jump Street* actors was video-captured in real time with a JVC ¾-inch videotape camera. The scanned image was then manipulated with Lumena 8 on an IBM computer.

Brownwood is an Anaheim-based freelance illustrator who uses the IBM and Macintosh. He does research and development for and is in charge of the computer graphics lab at STS Graphics, a screen printing company.

These two **Untitled** works (above and right) by Los Angeles artist **Paul Binkley** are combinations of scanned images, work done in paint programs and elements generated by mathematical processes such as cellular automata and fractals. Both were done on the Amiga 500 with DigiView, PhotonPaint, DigiPaint and a variety of public domain mathematical generation programs. They were output as 35mm transparencies by Philadelphia Video Lab by a proprietary process.

8-bit color — a description of systems that allocate 8 bits of information for each *pixel* (spot) in the image. This provides 256 possible colors or levels of gray. (Black-and-white systems are 1-bit.)

24-bit color — a description of systems that allocate 24 bits of data to each *pixel* (spot) in the image. Usually, the bits are allocated as 8 bits each for the three additive primary colors (red, green and blue). That arrangement provides over 16.7 million color possibilities.

accuracy — as applied to scanners, the closeness of the values reported for each spot in the image. Most scanners are specified as providing a number of digits of accuracy slightly less than the number of bits reported for each pixel. Thus a scanner that reports 8 bits per pixel might only claim 6 bits per pixel of accuracy.

additive color mixing — producing colors by mixing colors of light (red, green and blue) rather than by mixing pigments (such as cyan, magenta, yellow and black used in printing). See also *subtractive color mixing*.

alpha channel — **1.** in video systems in general, and particularly the new 32-bit color system recently adopted by Apple, an extra signal or set of bits that provides control information. Alpha-channel information is used primarily for controlling special effects such as transparency and overlay. **2.** in some graphics programs, a grayscale version of an image used to make special effects.

anamorphic — a change in size of an object such that it is stretched or compressed more in one dimension than another.

antialiasing — in video and graphics, efforts to smooth the appearance of jagged lines (jaggies) created by the limited resolution of a graphics system. The most common antialiasing technique is to add extra dots (phantom pixels) at random points adjacent to sloping lines or to use shading to simulate partial dots.

auto scroll — on some drawing and graphics programs, a feature that appears to move a large document to make more of it visible on the screen when the mouse pointer or a tool reaches the edge of the visible region.

autotrace, automatic trace — a mode on some drawing programs that creates a set of vectors to represent apparent outlines on a bitmapped image. It is used to create draw-style images for graphics programs starting from a paint-style image. Often the original is an image created by scanning a hand-drawn image.

baud — a measure of data transmission speed equal to the number of signal changes per second. For scanners attached directly to a computer via a serial port, it is equal to the bit rate (number of bits per second). Both scanner and serial port must be set to the same bit rate for the connection to work correctly.

bitmap — a type of graphics format in which the image is made up of a large number of tiny dots (bits) arranged on a closely spaced grid.

bits/pixel — a description of the number of levels of information a system stores about each point in an image. For every extra bit, the number of available colors or shades of gray doubles. Also called *pixel depth*.

blend — a feature on many digital painting programs that lets you soften the edges or mix colors where two objects or regions meet.

brightness — the perceived amount of light emitted or reflected by an object.

byte — 8 binary bits of data grouped together to store a character, digit or other value. The term was popularized by IBM in connection with their 360 Series computers, and is now universally used in the industry. In most recent devices, each byte can be used to store one character of alphanumeric data, so the size of such items in memory can be interchangeably given in bytes or characters.

cast — **1.** a tint or overemphasis of one color in a color image, particularly an unintended one. Also called *color cast.* **2.** in some Macintosh animation programs, the elements that can be moved around the screen.

CCD — an abbreviation for *charge-coupled device,* a type of light-sensitive computer chip used in scanners and some video cameras. CCDs come in a range of sizes, but since none have enough individual light-sensitive elements to convert a page-sized image in detail, they are usually combined with some type of mechanical scanning system for higher effective resolution.

chroma — **1.** in general, color (hue) information. **2.** with respect to video signals, the portion of the signal that carries the color information.

chroma key — a color-based video matting (overlay) system that drops all areas of a selected color (usually blue) out of the foreground image, and substitutes instead the corresponding areas of a second image. This allows a person in a studio standing before a blue background to appear to be standing in front of a weather map or any other image. Similar computer systems are often called *color key.*

chrome — a color transparency, particularly one larger than a 35mm slide.

clip — **1.** (also *crop*) to select a part of a graphic to show on the screen or place into a document; clipping is used to select a region of interest rather than scaling the entire image, or to prevent the possible confusion that might be caused if the image were allowed to overflow its area or wrap around from one edge of the screen to the other. **2.** to cut off the extreme part of a value, such as the extremes of color or brightness.

closed path — **1.** a path that returns to its starting point. **2.** a complete loop.

CLUT — see *color lookup table.*

CMYK — a color model based on the cyan, magenta, yellow and black inks used in color printing. The first three inks are used to form all the available colors by subtractive color mixing, while the black is used to change tones or define edges.

color correction — the process of changing the color balance of an image to more closely approach the desired values. Images are color-corrected to make up for the differences between the response of the film and ink and the human eye and to compensate for the effects of the printing process.

color lookup table (CLUT) — an ordered list of active colors (or pointers to color values) for use in a graphic display, where each color in the list is selected from a much larger possible set (the palette). Because the lookup table is much smaller than the full color palette, it takes fewer bits to describe each color, a factor that becomes important when displays use from thousands to millions of bits.

color model — a method for representing colors, usually by their components as specified along at least three dimensions. Common models include RGB (using red, green and blue light), HLS (hue, lightness and saturation), HSV (hue, saturation and value) and CMYK (using the common printing colors of cyan, magenta, yellow and black).

color separation — the process of dividing a colored image into a corresponding series of single-color images. Since color printing is done by printing four single-color images, color pictures and drawings must first be made into separate images for each of these colors (cyan, magenta, yellow and black). Until recently, color separation was done by photographing the image three times through different color filters. Most computerized separation systems work on the digital representation of the image rather than a photo.

color space — an imaginary area or volume containing all the points whose positions represent the available colors in a system when those points are graphed on a set of axes. Color spaces are associated with companion color models, such as HLS, HSV and RGB.

color spectrum — the range of colors available on a particular device or system, usually presented in the same order as the colors in the normal visible spectrum.

color wheel — a diagram in circular form that shows hue (color) as the angle around the circle and saturation as the distance from the center; colors opposite each other are complements.

Color Key — **1.** a proof sheet showing one of the colors of a color printing job. **2.** a 3M brand name for proofs made with a system of color-sensitive acetate overlays.

comp — as used in graphic arts, short for comprehensive layout; this is a mock-up of the final product made by sketching in the headlines, blocks of text and illustrations all in the correct size and position. Some newer page layout systems can produce a sort of automated comprehensive, using blocks or wavy lines in place of the planned text.

complement — referring to colors, the matching color that will combine with a specified original color to make white for light, or black for pigments; complement pairs are opposite each other on the color wheel, and can be paired for contrast or vibrancy.

constrain — to place limits on an operation, its inputs or the results. Drawing operations are often deliberately constrained by various options to produce circles, squares or vertical or horizontal lines.

continuous tone — said of a photograph or illustration containing a range or gradation of tones in black-and-white or color. Continuous-tone images cannot be reproduced by most printing or digital display technologies, which either place ink or color at a given point or do not. Consequently, images with such tones must be broken up into small dark and light areas or series of different colored dots. See also *screen, halftone* and *dither pattern.*

contrast — **1.** the ratio in brightness between the lightest part of an image and the darkest part. High contrast is desirable in computer displays and printed text, but excessive contrast causes eyestrain. For pictorial and graphic matter, too little contrast causes the picture to look dull or flat, while too much makes the picture seem stark and overexposed. **2.** in letterforms, the differences in thickness and darkness between parts of the letters. Some typefaces have a lot of contrast, while others are more even-toned. **3.** in layouts, the changes in brightness between different areas of the page or spread. Too little contrast produces a dull, flat-looking page, while too much may look garish. **4.** the control on a video display that alters the ratio of brightest to darkest part of the image; it should not be confused with the brightness control, which makes all areas brighter.

cool — referring to color images, ones that have a bluish tint; also called *cold.* Those that are more red are referred to as *warm.*

device driver — a special section of computer code that translates the more general commands from an operating system or user program into the exact code needed by a specific peripheral device. Most scanning programs use a set of several device drivers to control a number of different scanners.

digitizing resolution — the fineness of detail that a scanner can distinguish. Unless otherwise stated, it is the spatial resolution, reported in dots per linear inch (or dots per mm in metric areas).

direct color — said of systems that store an actual color value for each point or object in an image rather than using a color lookup table; sometimes called *true color.*

dither — to place small dots of black, white or one or more colors in an area of an image to soften an edge, to visually smooth a jagged line, or to simulate a shade, tone or intermediate tone.

dither pattern — for a scanner, a pattern of dots used to simulate gray tones or intermediate colors. Also called screen pattern.

DMA — an abbreviation for *direct memory access,* the transfer of data to and from memory without routing through the central processing unit (CPU) chip. Some scanner and computer combinations can use DMA for faster transfer of image data.

dots/mm — short for *dots per millimeter,* a unit of measure for the digitizing resolution of scanners and other graphics systems.

download — **1.** to send a file from a larger or remote computer to a smaller or local one. **2.** for scanners, to send operating instructions, parameter values or programs from a computer to the scanner.

dpi — an abbreviation for *dots per inch*, a measure of the resolution of printers and other output devices.

drive — the mechanism inside a scanner that moves the scanning head or image carrier to present each portion of the image to the scanning element.

driver — short for *device driver.*

electronic halftoning — to simulate shades of gray by using patterns of black and white dots.

enlargement — a proportional copy of an image that is larger than the original.

EPS, EPSF — short for *encapsulated PostScript format*, a combination of PostScript page description language statements needed to create a PostScript image, along with an optional bitmap version for quicker display.

feather — to blend or smooth the edge of a region or shape into a background or other object, especially in a slightly irregular fashion to achieve a natural-looking effect.

fill — **1.** a color or pattern occupying a defined region **2.** to place color or pattern in a region.

flatbed scanner — an input device for turning visible images into electronic equivalents; the user places the original face down against a flat plate of glass.

flip — to reverse an image side to side (to flip horizontally) or top to bottom (to flip vertically).

four-color — said of printing processes that use the three subtractive primary colors (cyan, yellow and magenta) plus black to create full-color images; also called *process color.*

gamma — an index number standing for the relation of illumination to response. Technically, it is the slope of the line that graphs that relation.

gamma correction — changing the way an image is captured, transferred or displayed by modifying the shape of the gamma *histogram* or curve. This is done mostly to improve the appearance of images with improper contrast or color balance.

GCR — short for *gray component replacement*, a technique for reducing the amount of cyan, magenta or yellow not only in a neutral area but also in a colored area and replacing it with an appropriate level of black. GCR is based on the fact that the first two colors in a mixture determine the hue and the third color (cyan, magenta or yellow) serves only as a darkening agent and can therefore be effectively replaced with black.

GPIB — an abbreviation for *general purpose interface bus,* a type of parallel interface sometimes used for connecting scanners to specialized computers.

gradient fill, graduated fill — a feature on some graphics programs that adds color or a shade of gray to a region, varying the color or shade smoothly in a defined direction.

grayscale mode — a scanner setting for digitizing an image made up of grays or intermediate colors by assigning more than 1 bit of data to each point. Other possibilities are *halftone* and *line-art* modes.

halftone — the technique of showing shades of intensity by combining differing sizes of tiny full-intensity dots. This is the method used to reproduce tones in most kinds of printing, since the printing process can only deposit or not deposit ink at any given point.

halftone mode — a scanner setting for digitizing an image made up of grays or intermediate colors by creating patterns of dots to simulate shading. Other possibilities are *grayscale* and *line-art* modes.

highlight — the lightest area on an image being photographed (and therefore the darkest area on the negative).

histogram — a chart showing the distribution of color or brightness in an image. Histograms are used mainly to provide the information needed for adjusting the settings of scanners or the characteristics of graphics filters in image editing.

host — in reference to a scanner or other peripheral, the computer to which it is attached.

host adapter — **1.** a board or circuit that connects a specific model of computer to a peripheral device or a more general controller. Some scanners require host adapters to connect to popular desktop computers. **2.** a board or unit that connects a computer to a standard interface. For example, a board that connects a PC to a SCSI interface.

hot — as applied to images, very bright or excessively bright.

hotspot — the point or region on a graphic, icon or cursor that is active, responding to inputs or representing the position of the object.

HSV — short for *hue, saturation* and *value,* a color model used in some graphics programs. HSV has to be translated to another model for colored printing or for actually forming screen colors.

hue — the property of color corresponding to the frequency or wavelength of the light. This is what makes red different from green or purple different from yellow, for example.

image compression — as applied to scanners and graphics computer systems, encoding the data describing an image in a more compact form to reduce storage requirements or transmission time.

imagesetter — a high-resolution output device used to set type and pictures. Most current models use a laser to write the image directly on photosensitive film or paper.

indexed color — a color system that uses information from the user or from programs as a pointer to a table of output colors, rather than specifying the color directly. This is the system used in the Macintosh for *8-bit color,* allowing programs to pick up to 256 colors at a time from a palette of over 16.7 million possibilities.

jaggies — the jagged edges formed on raster scan displays of diagonal lines. See *antialiasing* for more details.

landscape — an orientation for paper or a rectangular image with the long way horizontal. The complementary orientation is called *portrait.*

lasso — on many graphics programs, a tool that selects irregularly shaped regions from the image for further processing.

line art — illustrations containing only blacks and whites, with no intermediate tones (or similarly, a bitonal arrangement of some other color). Line art can be reproduced without the screening or patterning step most printing processes need to produce a range of tones.

line-art mode — a scanner setting for digitizing an image by characterizing each point either as black or white with no shades of gray. Other possibilities are *halftone* and *grayscale* modes. See *threshold.*

lpi — an abbreviation for *lines per inch,* a figure used to indicate the spacing of the dots making up a halftone screen.

luminance — **1.** the intensity of a light source or object. **2.** in video signals, the intensity signal without the color information.

marquee — a rectangular area, often bounded by blinking dashes or dotted lines, used to select objects or regions in a drawing program.

mask — **1.** to block out part of an image, either to get rid of unwanted detail or to facilitate the addition of another image. **2.** to block out part of an image or deselect it so it won't be affected by a change or operation. **3.** a shape or region used to block out part of an image for the above purposes.

moiré — a type of interference pattern created when two or more images with regularly spaced features overlap. Through proper adjustment of images and selection of patterns, moiré dots and lines can be minimized.

monochrome — **1.** literally one color, but in practice a single color plus black. **2.** the term is often used to describe monitors that show images in black-and-white (or black-and-green or black-and-amber).

montage — **1.** a composite image, especially one made up of elements that are distinct or would normally not be placed together. **2.** a type of video sequence made up of many short images where the symbolic meaning of the images or their relations are the message, rather than any literal temporal or spatial sequence.

OCR — see *optical character recognition*.

opacity — **1.** as applied to paper, the amount that it prevents an image on the reverse side or an adjacent sheet from showing through. **2.** as applied to a graphic element, the degree to which an element will hide anything in layers below it.

optical character recognition (OCR) — the process of having a computer translate images of text into the corresponding computer codes.

sheet-fed scanner — a graphics or OCR scanner that includes a mechanism for feeding in multiple sheets of paper under computer control.

paint — **1.** as applied to graphics programs, one that treats an image as a collection of individual dots or picture elements (pixels) rather than as a composition of a shape. **2.** on many drawing programs, to give a path or shape visible characteristics, such as by filling it with color or gray or giving weight and color to the path.

palette — the collection of colors or shades available to a graphics system or program. On many systems, the number of colors available for use at any time is limited to a selection from the overall system palette.

Pantone Matching System — also known as *PMS*, a system of color samples, licensed coloring materials and standards developed by Pantone, Inc. for use in specifying and checking colors for reproduction.

parallel interface — a connection that sends the bits making up data across several lines at once. This type of connection is usually limited to short distances, but it is faster than the alternative seria*l interface*.

PCX (picture exchange) — the file format produced by Z-Soft's PC Paintbrush and other programs to save paint-style images. It is also used by many scanners.

photorealistic — said of images that look like they could have been produced by a photographic process. For a computer image, this usually means one with good spatial resolution, sufficient color depth (number of colors) and accurate rendition of a real or imaginary object.

pica — a printing-industry unit of measure, equal to approximately ⅙ of an inch. There are 12 points to a pica. Pica measurements are often used for the width and sometimes height of page areas and columns of type.

PICT — the standard file format used to pass images back and forth between Macintosh applications and the main format used by the clipboard. PICT files consist of collections of the Macintosh QuickDraw routines needed to create the image.

pixel — short for *picture element*, the smallest object or dot that can be changed in a display or on a printed page.

pixel depth — the number of levels of information a system stores about each point in an image. For every extra bit, the number of colors or shades of gray doubles. The most common unit is *bits/pixel*.

place — to put a block of type or pictorial element at a particular position on a page in a page layout program.

PMS — see *Pantone Matching System*.

portrait — in describing image orientation, complement of *landscape*.

posterize — to transform an image to a more stark form by rounding tonal or color values to a small number of possible values.

PostScript — **1.** a trademark of Adobe Systems, Inc. for the firm's page description language used to describe images and type in a machine-independent form. **2.** loosely used to refer to the interpreter program that translates PostScript language files to the actual sequences of machine operations needed to produce an output image.

PostScript Level 2 — an updated version of the PostScript language that adds support for color, forms handling, data compression and many other features.

preprocessing — the steps that may be used on an image between the capturing of the image and any analysis. Typically, preprocessing might include averaging, contrast enhancement and so on.

primary — as applied to colors, the minimum set of colors that can be mixed to produce the full color range. For inks the colors are yellow, magenta and cyan; for light they are red, green and blue; for pigments they are red, yellow and blue.

process-color — see *four-color*.

progressive proofs — the sequence of proofs (test images) showing how a printed color image looks as each ink color is added to the image. Traditionally, a full set includes one proof of each color plus the successive combinations of yellow/magenta, yellow/magenta/cyan, and yellow/magenta/cyan/black.

QuickDraw — an Apple trademark for the set of drawing routines provided by the Macintosh operating system. The routines can be used by individual programs, and are also used as the basis for the PICT file format.

raster image file format — also known as *RIFF*, a file format for graphics developed by Letraset USA that is an expanded version of the TIFF format used by many scanner makers.

rasterize — to change a drawing held in a drawing or CAD system in vector (line and shape) form to the raster (collection of individual pixels) form used by most video displays and printers.

reflect — to make a mirror image of an object around a specified point or line.

reflection copy — material to be scanned that has an opaque base and that is imaged by catching the light bounced back from the front surface, as opposed to a transparent original.

regeneration — the production of a new screen image after a change in scale, position or elements; also called *screen refresh*.

register — **1.** the alignment of the printed image with its intended position on the page. **2.** the alignment of parts of an image with other parts, especially with parts that are printed separately, as in color separation.

renderer — a program or function that takes a geometric model or description of a scene and produces the corresponding images. Usually, the renderer can add solid surfaces, tonal or color shading, transparency effects and so on.

render — to produce an image from a model or description. Usually, this means filling in a graphic object or image with color and brightness (or just shading for monochrome systems). Realistic rendering takes a lot of computing power and advanced techniques.

RenderMan — a Pixar trademark for that firm's line of software for drawing finished photorealistic images.

resolution — 1. in general, how many different values are distinguishable. 2. for graphics output, it's usually spatial resolution (the tightness of the spots making up an image), measured in dots or lines per inch. 3. for displays, it may be the output density (in dots or pixels per inch) or the screen resolution (measured in total dots wide by dots high) or the video resolution (measured in horizontal lines) or the color resolution (measured in the number of colors in the palette or the number available on-screen at any one time). 4. in typesetting, the size of the smallest change that can be accurately controlled or noted. Used mostly in conjunction with digital typesetters, which construct each character from bit patterns in memory. A finer resolution means smoother, sharper characters. 5. for television graphic systems, the ability to produce small details. It is usually specified as the rise time (transition time) of the edges measured in nanoseconds.

retouch — to change an image, especially by painting on a photographic negative.

RGB — 1. as a color model, a method of representing all colors as the combination of red, green and blue light that would create that color. The RGB color space is usually represented as a square, with one corner black and the opposing corner white. Although this model is mechanically simple and fits in well with RGB video systems, it is hard to work with artistically or conceptually. 2. as applied to video systems, short for red, green and blue, three color signals that can between them create a complete video image. RGB systems can be digital (each of the three signals can only assume a number of defined states) or analog (each signal can vary smoothly over its range). 3. a characterization of video systems that work with picture information carried on three signal (red, green, blue) lines rather than combined in a single line (composite color).

RIFF — see *raster image file format*.

rotate — to revolve an object around a specified point.

saturation — when referring to colors, the extent to which a color is made purely of a selected hue rather than a mixture of that color and white. It is the property that makes pale pink different from bright red of the same hue.

scale — 1. to change in size, particularly to change proportionally in both dimensions. 2. the amount by which an image should be enlarged or reduced. 3. as applied to type, to change in size proportionately, and in many cases to adjust the resulting character forms to fit the new size.

scan — 1. to convert an image from visible form to an electronic description. Most available systems turn the image into a corresponding series of dots but do not actually recognize shapes. However, some attempt to group the dots into their corresponding characters (optical character recognition) or corresponding objects. 2. particularly, to use a scanner (an input device containing a camera or photosensitive element) to produce an electronic image of an object or of the contents of a sheet of paper. 3. a scanned image.

scanned image — an image in bitmap form produced by a scanner. Many layout programs can scale or crop scanned images before placing them into a page.

scanner — 1. an input device that converts a drawing or illustration into a corresponding electronic bitmap image. In the graphic arts industry, sometimes called an *illustration scanner*. 2. an input device that converts a page or section of text into the corresponding characters in memory or a computer file. Also called an *OCR (optical character recognition) scanner*.

scanning area — the dimensions of the largest original image that can be captured by a particular scanner. On most models, it is slightly smaller than the maximum paper size.

scanning time — the interval a system needs to convert a visible image to an electronic equivalent. Specified values usually omit any needed warmup time before a first image or the time needed to feed in or position the image for scanning.

scrapbook — a special file on the Macintosh and some programs on other systems that is used to store copies of images or sections of text for possible use in documents.

screen — **1.** to take images that have continuous tones and break them up into patterns of tiny saturated dots, with the darker tones represented by larger or closer dots. This is a necessary step for most printing technologies, which cannot directly print intermediate tones; the dot pattern used in such a process. See also *halftone.* **2.** a ruled or patterned piece of film, glass or plastic used to break up an image in to a series of dots.

screen angle — the rotation of the direction of the lines or major direction of the pattern in the screen used for making halftones. In four-color process printing, the screen angle is usually set to 45 degrees for black, 75 degrees for magenta, 90 degrees for yellow and 105 degrees for cyan, or 45 degrees for black, 75 degrees for magenta, 15 degrees for cyan and 0 degrees for yellow.

screen frequency — the number of lines or dots in a stated distance for halftone (screened) images; often measured in lines per inch (lpi). A 60 lpi screen is very coarse, while a 200-line screen is fine.

screen refresh — see *regeneration.*

SCSI — pronounced "scuzzy"; short for *small computer system interface,* an industry-standard interface between computers and peripheral device controllers such as the controllers for a hard disk. All current models of the Macintosh include a SCSI connection, and SCSI interfaces are available for PC-style computers. SCSI connections allow high-speed data transfers and up to seven devices for each connection.

select — to choose an item or a location on-screen for the next action.

serial interface — a connection that sends the bits making up the data one after another down a single signal pathway. While easy to implement, this type of connection is usually slower than a *parallel interface.*

service life — the expected operating time before a component will wear out or fail. For scanners, seen particularly as a characteristic of the lamps used to illuminate the copy.

shade — a mixture of a pure color plus black.

shading — **1.** as applied to graphic objects, the way light reflects off a surface. **2.** changing the brightness and color of parts of an image to simulate depth or otherwise enhance definition. Common techniques include facet shading, linear shading, Gouraud shading, Phong shading and ray tracing.

shadow — **1.** the darkest area of an image that is being photographed, and therefore the lightest area on the negative. **2.** as a graphics tool, one that inserts a partial copy or dark outline behind a selected object, producing the appearance of a shadow.

sharpen — an image enhancement that increases the apparent sharpness of an image by increasing the contrast of edges. Actually, the effect further distorts an image and its repetitive use on the same signal will create a less realistic image.

shear — in painting and drawing programs, to slant an object along a specified axis (much the way a type of simple italic might be made by slanting a normal upright roman character).

smudge — a feature on some graphics programs that blends colors or softens edges that are already in place in an image. The effect is supposed to resemble what would happen if the image was made of wet paint and you ran a finger over the area.

solarize — to change the intensity levels in an image in a way that particularly brightens or transforms the middle levels.

spot — **1.** in referring to the output of an imagesetter or film recorder, the smallest element that can be written. Also called a *dot* or *pixel*. **2.** to retouch a small area of an image, particularly using a brush.

spot color — color that is applied only as individually specified areas of a single ink color; compare *process color,* whereby colors may be mixed and each dot of printed color must be determined by a more complex overall color-separation process.

stitch — to combine several images, especially combining side-by-side strips made by hand scanners, into a single image.

subtractive color mixing — producing colors by combining pigments (such as cyan, magenta, yellow and black used in printing) or other colorants to absorb light. See also *additive color mixing.*

subtractive primaries — the three process printing ink colors that can form all other colors (except pure white) when mixed together in the right ratios. They are cyan, magenta and yellow.

tagged image file format — also called *TIFF* for short; a file format developed by Aldus and Microsoft to represent bitmap images, particularly those produced by scanners. TIFF is an open-ended standard with several variants: uncompressed TIFF essentially is a bitmap of the image; compressed TIFF formats use encoding methods to remove redundant information from the file; grayscale TIFF includes information about the lightness of each point (normally from among 64 or 256 levels); and screened or halftone TIFF carries tonal information represented as patterns of black dots and white dots.

template — **1.** a document or image used to establish the format of new documents. **2.** an image used as a base or guide, particularly one used to trace over.

termination — a type of electronic "shock absorber" that must be added to some connections such as SCSI links to prevent electronic noise and ringing.

threshold — **1.** in general, a limit or standard used to divide values into classes. **2.** in scanning line art, a value used as a standard for whether a particular spot should be considered black or white. **3.** to collapse the range of values into an image to those falling above or below a selected standard.

TIFF — see *tagged image file format.*

TIFF-24 — a version of the *tagged image file format* (TIFF) that encodes 24 bits of information for each point in the image.

tile — **1.** to fill an area with small, regular shapes, creating an effect that looks like a wall surfaced with individual tiles. **2.** the individual shape that is repeated to fill an area. **3.** a single sheet or portion that will be combined with others to assemble an oversize page. **4.** a method of showing multiple windows on a display screen that puts images side-by-side instead of overlapping the windows like a stack of paper (called *overlapped windows*).

tint — **1.** a mixture of a particular color plus white. **2.** a solid area of color, particularly one of a specific hue but at less than full intensity or saturation. **3.** in printing, a light or screened color applied over an area.

tonal range — the spread between the lightest and darkest parts of an image.

toolbox — **1.** a set of standard routines provided by a program or operating system that can be called on by other programs or by the user. **2.** an on-screen array of images representing these routines.

transmission copy — material that is scanned by capturing the light that passes through it. Also called *transparent copy.* See *reflection copy.*

transparency — for a graphics object or image, the attribute of letting an underlying image show through. Transparency can be partial or total.

true color — **1.** color systems in which the color information in the image is used directly to create the output color rather than as an index to a table of colors in a palette. **2.** said of color systems that have enough available colors to make the choices seem continuous to the human eye; 24-bit color (about 16 million available colors) is usually considered to be true color.

undercolor removal (UCR) — A technique for reducing the amount of magenta, yellow and cyan in neutral areas by removing equal amounts of each and replacing them with the equivalent amount of black. Three times as much total color is removed as the amount of black added.

value — regarding color or shades of gray, the degree of lightness or darkness.

warm — referring to color images, ones that have a reddish tint. Those that are more blue are referred to as *cool* or *cold*.

window — a selected portion of a file or image displayed on-screen.

windowing — referring to software for scanners, a feature that allows the user to select only part of a page or image for conversion to digital form.

zoom — **1.** to change the size of the area selected for viewing or display to provide either a more detailed view or more of an overview. Some systems allow any amount of zoom, while others only zoom in discrete steps. **2.** in computer graphics, to change the apparent magnification or scale factor of a region, window or display to provide a more detailed view or more of an overview.

Resources

This appendix lists software, hardware and other resources of use to artists working with scanned imagery. The resources are grouped in categories in the following order:

Image-Processing Software

Paint Programs

Clip Art

Graphics Tablets

Scanners

Video Digitizers and Frame Grabbers

Still Video

Storage Systems

Monitors

Color Calibration

Accelerators

3D Programs

PostScript Illustration Software

Draw Programs

Page Layout Programs

Fonts

Utilities, Desk Accessories and INITs

Prepress Systems

Printers and Imagesetters

Large-Format Output Services

Film Recorders

Periodicals

Books

Bulletin Board Services

Communication Software

Image-Processing Software

Adobe Photoshop
Adobe Systems, Inc.
PO Box 7900
Mountain View, CA 94039-7900
800-344-8335

ColorStudio
Letraset USA
40 Eisenhower Drive
Paramus, NJ 07653
201-845-6100

Digital Darkroom
Silicon Beach Software
9770 Carroll Center Road, Suite J
San Diego, CA 92126
619-695-6956

Enhance
MicroFrontier, Inc.
7650 Hickman Road
Des Moines, IA 50322
800-388-8109

Gray F/X
Xerox Imaging Systems, Inc.
535 Oakmead Parkway
Sunnyvale, CA 94086
408-245-7900

Hercules Art Department
Hercules Computer Technology
921 Parker Street
Berkeley, CA 94710
415-540-6000

ImageStudio
Letraset USA
40 Eisenhower Drive
Paramus, NJ 07653
201-845-6100

PhotoMac
Data Translation
100 Locke Drive
Marlboro, MA 01752
508-481-3700

Picture Publisher
Astral Development Corporation
Londonderry Square, Suite 112
Londonderry, NH 03053
603-432-6800

Targa TIPS
Truevision
7340 Shadeland Station
Indianapolis, IN 4625-3935
317-841-0332

Paint Programs

Color MacCheese
Delta Tao Software
760 Howard Avenue
Sunnyvale, CA 94087
408-730-9336

DeluxePaint 3.0
Electronic Arts
1820 Gateway Drive
San Mateo, CA 94404
415-571-7171

DigiPaint
NewTek
115 W. Crane Street
Topeka, KS 66603
800-843-8934

GraphicWorks
MacroMind, Inc.
410 Townsend Avenue, Suite 408
San Francisco, CA 94107
415-442-0200

LaserPaint
LaserWare
PO Box 668
San Rafael, CA 94915
800-367-6898

Lumena
Time Arts, Inc.
1425 Corporate Center Parkway
Santa Rosa, CA 95407
415-576-7722

MacPaint
Claris Corporation
440 Clyde Avenue
Mountain View, CA 94043
415-962-8946

PC Paintbrush IV Plus
ZSoft Corporation
450 Franklin Road, Suite 100
Marietta, GA 30067
404-428-0008

PhotonPaint
MicroIllusions
10815 Zelzah Avenue
Granada Hills, CA 91344
818-360-3715

PixelPaint 2.0
SuperMac Technology
485 Potrero Avenue
Sunnyvale, CA 94086
408-245-0022

PixelPaint Professional
SuperMac Technology
485 Potrero Avenue
Sunnyvale, CA 94086
408-245-0022

Studio/8
Electronic Arts, Inc.
1820 Gateway Drive
San Mateo, CA 94404
415-571-7171

Studio/32
Electronic Arts, Inc.
1820 Gateway Drive
San Mateo, CA 94404
415-571-7171

SuperPaint 2.0
Silicon Beach Software
9770 Carroll Center Road, Suite J
San Diego, CA 92126
619-695-6956

UltraPaint
Deneba Software
7855 N.W. 12th Street
Miami, FL 33126
800-622-6827

VideoPaint
Olduvai Corporation
7520 Red Road, Suite A
South Miami, FL 33143
305-665-4665

Clip Art

Comstock Desktop Photography
Comstock, Inc.
30 Irving Place
New York, NY 10003
212-353-8686

Darkroom CD-ROM
Image Club Graphics
1902 11th Street S.E., Suite 5
Calgary, AB T2G 3G2 Canada
800-661-9410

Photo Gallery
NEC Technologies, Inc.
1414 Massachusetts Avenue
Boxborough, MA 01719
508-264-8000

PhotoFiles
GoldMind Publishing
4994 Tulsa Avenue
Riverside, CA 92505
714-687-3815

Professional Photography Collection
disc*Imagery*
18 E. 16th Street
New York, NY 10003
212-675-8500

The Right Images
(Vol. 1, Photoclip Collection)
Tsunami Press
275 Route 18
E. Brunswick, NJ 08816
201-613-0509

Graphics Tablets

Kurta
3007 E. Chambers
Phoenix, AZ 85040
602-276-5533

Summagraphics Corporation
325 Heights Road
Houston, TX 77007
713-869-7009

Wacom, Inc.
West 115 Century Road
Paramus, NJ 07652
201-265-4226

Scanners

Abaton Scan 300/FB and 300/S
Abaton Technology Corporation
48431 Milmont Drive
Fremont, CA 94538
415-683-2226

Apple Scanner
Apple Computer, Inc.
20525 Mariani Avenue
Cupertino, CA 95014
408-996-1010

C1S-3513 35mm Scanning System
Barneyscan Corporation
1125 Atlantic Avenue
Alameda, CA 94501
415-521-3388

ClearScan
NCL
1221 Innsbruck Drive
Sunnyvale, CA 94089
408-734-1006

Dest PC Scan 1000 and 2000 series
Dest Corporation
1201 Cadillac Court
Milpitas, CA 95035
408-946-7100

Eikonix 1435 slide scanner
Atex Magazine Publishing Systems
32 Wiggins Avenue
Bedford, MA 01730
617-276-7195

Howtek ScanMaster II
Howtek
21 Park Avenue
Hudson, NH 03051
603-882-5200

HP ScanJet Plus
Hewlett-Packard Company
700 71st Avenue
Greeley, CO 80634
303-845-4045

JX-100, JX-300, JX-450 and JX-600
Color Scanners
Sharp Electronics
Sharp Plaza, Box C Systems
Mahwah, NJ 07430
201-529-8200

LightningScan 400
Thunderware, Inc.
21 Orinda Way
Orinda, CA 94563
415-254-6581

LS-3500 slide scanner
Nikon Electronic Imaging
623 Stewart Avenue
Garden City, NY 11530
516-222-0200

Microtek Scanners
Microtek Labs, Inc.
16901 S. Western Avenue
Gardena, CA 90247
213-321-2121

ScanMan Plus hand-held scanner
Logitech
6505 Kaiser Drive
Fremont, CA 94555
415-795-8500

Silverscanner
LaCie
19552 S.W. 90th Court
Tualatin, OR 97062
800-999-0143

Thunderscan
Thunderware, Inc.
21 Orinda Way
Orinda, CA 94563
415-254-6581

Video Digitizers and Frame Grabbers

ColorCapture
Data Translation, Inc.
100 Locke Drive
Marlboro, MA 01725

ColorSnap 32
Computer Friends, Inc.
14250 N.W. Science Park Drive
Portland, OR 97220
800-547-3303

ColorSpace
Mass Microsystems
550 Del Rey Avenue
Sunnyvale, CA 94086
800-522-7979

ComputerEyes
Digital Vision, Inc.
270 Bridge Street
Dedham, MA 02026
617-329-5400

DigiView
NewTek
115 W. Crane Street
Topeka, KS 66603
800-843-8934

Eikonix 1412 Digital Imaging System
Atex Magazine Publishing Systems
32 Wiggins Avenue
Bedford, MA 01730
617-276-7195

Frame Grabber 324 NC
RasterOps
2500 Walsh Avenue
Santa Clara, CA 95051
800-468-7600

MacVision video digitizer
Koala Technologies
70 N. Second Street
San Jose, CA 95113
408-438-0946

Neotech Image Grabber
Advent Computer Products, Inc.
449 Santa Fe Drive, Suite 213
Encinitas, CA 92024
619-942-8456

NuVista+
Truevision, Inc.
7340 Shadeland Station
Indianapolis, IN 46256-0332
317-576-7700

PC-Eye Video Digitizers and PC Frame Grabbers
Chorus Data Systems, Inc.
6 Continental Boulevard
Merrimack, NH 03054
603-424-2900

Quick Capture
Data Translation, Inc.
100 Locke Drive
Marlboro, MA 01752
508-481-3700

Quick Image 24
Mass Microsystems
550 Del Rey Avenue
Sunnyvale, CA 94086
800-522-7979

Radius TV
Radius, Inc.
1710 Fortune Drive
San Jose, CA 95131
800-527-1950

TV Producer
Computer Friends, Inc.
14250 Science Park Drive
Portland, OR 97229
800-547-3303

WTI Moonraker
Advent Computer Products, Inc.
449 Santa Fe Drive, Suite 213
Encinitas, CA 92024
619-942-8456

Still Video

Canon Xapshot still video camera
Canon RC-470 frame-mode camera
Canon RV-301 and FV-540 players
Canon RP-420 printer
Canon USA
1 Canon Plaza
Lake Success, NY 11042
516-488-6700

Sony Mavica cameras
Sony MAP-T2 adapter
Sony MVP-660 player
Sony UP-5000 printer
Sony Corporation of America
9901 Business Parkway
Lanham, MD 20706
301-577-4850

Storage Systems

FWB, Inc.
2040 Polk Street, Suite 215
San Francisco, CA 94109
415-474-8055

Iomega Corporation
1821 W. 4000th S.
Roy, UT 84067
800-456-5522

Jasmine Technology, Inc.
1740 Army Street
San Francisco, CA 94124
415-282-1111

Storage Dimensions
2145 Hamilton Avenue
San Jose, CA 95125
408-879-0300

LaCie
19552 S.W. 90th Court
Tualitin, OR 97062
800-999-0143

Mass Microsystems
550 Del Rey Avenue
Sunnyvale, CA 94086
800-522-7979

OCEAN Microsystems, Inc.
246 E. Hacienda Avenue
Campbell, CA 95008
800-262-3261

Pinnacle Micro
15265 Alton Parkway
Irvine, CA 92718
714-727-3300

PLI
47421 Bayside Parkway
Fremont, CA 94538
415-657-2211

Sumo Systems
1580 Old Oakland Road, Suite C103
San Jose, CA 95131
408-453-5744

SuperMac Technology
485 Potrero Avenue
Sunnyvale, CA 94086
408-245-2202

Transitional Technology
5401 E. La Palma Avenue
Anaheim, CA 92807
714-693-1133

Monitors

Amdek Corporation
3471 N. First Street
San Jose, CA 95134
800-722-6335

Apple Computer, Inc.
20525 Mariani Avenue
Cupertino, CA 95014
408-996-1010

E-Machines, Inc.
9305 S.W. Gemini Drive
Beaverton, OR 97005
503-646-6699

MegaGraphics, Inc.
439 Calle San Pablo
Camarillo, CA 93010
805-484-3799

Mitsubishi Electronics
991 Knox Street
Torrance, CA 90502
213-217-5732

Moniterm Corporation
5740 Green Circle Drive
Minnetonka, MN 55343
612-935-4151

Nutmeg Systems, Inc.
25 South Avenue
New Canaan, CT 06840
800-777-8439

Radius, Inc.
1710 Fortune Drive
San Jose, CA 95131
408-434-1010

RasterOps Corporation
2500 Walsh Avenue
Santa Clara, CA 95051
408-562-4200

SuperMac Technology
485 Potrero Avenue
Sunnyvale, CA 94086
408-245-0022

Color Calibration

The Calibrator
Barco, Inc.
1500 Wilson Way, Suite 250
Smyrna, GA 30082
404-432-2346

PrecisionColor Calibrator
Radius, Inc.
1710 Fortune Drive
San Jose, CA 95131
408-434-1010

TekColor
Visual Systems Group
5770 Ruffin Road
San Diego, CA 92123
619-292-7330

Accelerators

Daystar Digital
5556 Atlanta Highway
Flowery Branch, GA 30542
404-967-2077

Radius, Inc.
1710 Fortune Drive
San Jose, CA 95131
408-434-0770

RasterOps Corp.
2500 Walsh Avenue
Santa Clara, CA 95051
408-562-4200

Siclone Sales & Engineering Corp.
107 Bonaventura Drive
San Jose, CA 95134
800-767-8207

3D Programs

AutoDesk 3D Studio
AutoDesk
2320 Marinship Way
Sausalito, CA 94965
415-332-2344

MacRenderMan
Pixar
3240 Kerner Boulevard
San Rafael, CA 94901
415-258-8100

MacroMind 3D
MacroMind, Inc.
410 Townsend Avenue, Suite 408
San Francisco, CA 94107
415-442-0200

Sculpt 3D
Byte by Byte
9442 Capital of Texas Highway N.
Austin, TX 78759
512-343-4357

StrataVision 3D
Strata
2 W. Saint George Boulevard
Ancestor Square, Suite 2100
Saint George, UT 84770
801-628-5218

Super 3D
Silicon Beach Software
9770 Carroll Center Road, Suite J
San Diego, CA 92126
619-695-6956

Swivel 3D
Paracomp, Inc.
1725 Montgomery Street, Second Floor
San Francisco, CA 94111
415-956-4091

Zing
Mindscape
3444 Dundee Road, Suite 203
Northbrook, IL 60062
708-480-7667

PostScript Illustration Software

Adobe Illustrator
Adobe Systems, Inc.
PO Box 7900
Mountain View, CA 94039-7900
800-344-8335

Adobe Streamline
Adobe Systems, Inc.
PO Box 7900
Mountain View, CA 94039-7900
800-344-8335

Aldus FreeHand
Aldus Corporation
411 First Avenue S.
Seattle, WA 98104
206-622-5500

Arts & Letters
Computer Support
15926 Midway Road
Dallas, TX 75244
214-661-8960

Corel Draw
Corel Systems Corporation
1600 Carling Avenue, Suite 190
Ottawa, ON K1Z 8R7 Canada
613-728-8200

Cricket Draw
Cricket Software
40 Valley Stream Parkway
Mallvern PA 19355
215-251-9890

Cricket Stylist
Computer Associates
10505 Sorrento Valley Road
San Diego, CA 92121-1698
619-452-00170

GEM Artline
Digital Research
70 Garden Court
Monterey, CA 93940
408-649-3896

Micrgrafx Designer
Micrografx
1303 Arapaho Road
Richardson, TX 75081-1769
800-272-3729

Smart Art, Volumes I, II, III
Emerald City Software
1040 Marsh Road, Suite 110
Menlo Park, CA 94025
415-324-8080

Draw Programs

Canvas
Deneba Software
7855 N.W. 12th Street
Miami, FL 33126
800-622-6827

MacDraw
Claris Corporation
440 Clyde Avenue
Mountain View, CA 94043
415-962-8946

Page Layout Programs

Aldus PageMaker
Aldus Corporation
411 First Avenue S.
Seattle, WA 98104
206-622-5500

DesignStudio
Letraset USA
40 Eisenhower Drive
Paramus, NJ 07653
201-845-6100

FrameMaker
Frame Technology Corporation
1010 Rincon Circle
San Jose, CA 95131
408-433-1928

Interleaf Publisher
Interleaf, Inc.
10 Canal Park
Cambridge, MA 02141
800-922-5675

Personal Press
Silicon Beach Software
9770 Carroll Center Road, Suite J
San Diego, CA 92126
619-695-6956

QuarkXPress
Quark, Inc.
300 S. Jackson Street, Suite 100
Denver, CO 80209
800-543-7711

Ventura Publisher
Xerox Product Support
1301 Ridgeview Drive
Lewisville, TX 75067
800-822-8221

Fonts

Adobe Type Library
Adobe Systems, Inc.
PO Box 7900
Mountain View, CA 94039-7900
800-344-8335

Bitstream fonts and
Fontware Installation Kit
Bitstream, Inc.
215 First Street
Cambridge, MA 02142
800-522-3668

CG Type
Agfa Compugraphic Division
90 Industrial Way
Wilmington, MA 01887
800-622-8973

Corel Headline, Corel Loader,
Corel Newfont
Corel Systems Corporation
1600 Carling Avenue, Suite 190
Ottawa, ON K1Z 8R7 Canada
613-728-8200

18+ Fonts
18+ Fonts
337 White Hall Terrace
Bloomingdale, IL 60108
312-980-0887

Em Dash fonts
Em Dash
PO Box 8256
Northfield, IL 60093
312-441-6699

Fluent Laser Fonts
Casady & Greene, Inc.
26080 Carmel Rancho Blvd., Suite 202
Carmel, CA 93923
800-359-4920

Font Factory Fonts (for LaserJet)
The Font Factory
13601 Preston Road, Suite 500-W
Dallas, TX 75240
214-239-6085

FontGen IV Plus
VS Software
PO Box 165920
Little Rock, AR 72216
501-376-2083

Font Solution Pack
SoftCraft, Inc.
16 N. Carroll Street, Suite 500
Madison, WI 53073
608-257-3300

Hewlett-Packard Soft Fonts
(for LaserJet)
Hewlett-Packard Company
PO Box 60008
Sunnyvale, CA 94088-60008
800-538-8787

Hot Type
Image Club Graphics Inc.
1902 11th Street S.E.
Calgary, AB T2G 3G2 Canada
800-661-9410

Kingsley/ATF typefaces
(ATF Classic type)
Type Corporation
2559-2 E. Broadway
Tucson, AZ 85716
800-289-8973

Laser fonts and font utilities
SoftCraft, Inc.
16 N. Carroll Street, Suite 500
Madison, WI 53703
800-351-0500

Laserfonts
Century Software/MacTography
326-D N. Stonestreet Avenue
Rockville, MD 20850
301-424-1357

Monotype fonts
Monotype Typography
53 W. Jackson Boulevard, Suite 504
Chicago, IL 60604
800-666-6897

Ornate Typefaces
Ingrimayne Software
PO Box 404
Rensselaer, IN 47978
219-866-6241

Treacyfaces Typeface Collection
Treacyfaces, Inc.
111 Sibley Avenue
Ardmore, PA 19003
215-896-0860

Typographic Ornaments
The Underground Grammarian
PO Box 203
Glassboro, NJ 08028
609-589-6477

URW fonts
The Font Company
12629 N. Tatum Boulevard, Suite 210
Phoenix, AZ 85032
800-442-3668

Varityper fonts
Tegra/Varityper
11 Mt. Pleasant Avenue
East Hanover, NJ 07936
201-884-6277

VS Library of Fonts
VS Software
PO Box 165920
Little Rock, AR 72216
501-376-2083

Utilities, Desk Accessories and INITs

Adobe Type Align
Adobe Systems, Inc.
PO Box 7900
Mountain View, CA 94039-7900
800-344-8335

Adobe Type Manager
Adobe Systems, Inc.
PO Box 7900
Mountain View, CA 94039-7900
800-344-8335

Adobe Type Reunion
Adobe Systems, Inc.
PO Box 7900
Mountain View, CA 94039-7900
800-344-8335

After Dark screen saver
Berkeley Systems, Inc.
1700 Shattuck Avenue
Berkeley, CA 94709
415-540-5535

Capture
Mainstay
5311-B Derry Avenue
Agoura Hills, CA 91301
818-991-6540

DaynaFile for Macintosh
Dayna Communications, Inc.
50 S. Main Street, Suite 530
Salt Lake City, UT 84144
800-531-0203

Diskfit
SuperMac Technology
485 Potrero Avenue
Sunnyvale, CA 94086
408-245-2202

DiskTools Plus
Electronic Arts
1820 Gateway Drive
San Mateo, CA 94404
800-245-4525

DOS Mounter
Dayna Communications, Inc.
50 S. Main Street, Suite 530
Salt Lake City, UT 84144
800-531-0203

Exposure
Preferred Publishers, Inc.
5100 Poplar Avenue, Suite 706
Memphis, TN 38137
901-683-3383

Fastback II
Fifth Generation Systems, Inc.
10049 Reiger Road
Baton Rouge, LA 70809
800-873-4384

Flowfazer
Utopia Grokware
300 Valley Street, Suite 204
Sausalito, CA 94965
415-331-0714

Font/DA Juggler Plus
Alsoft, Inc.
PO Box 927
Spring, TX 77383-0929
713-353-4090

InitPicker
Microseeds Publishing, Inc.
7030-B W. Hillsborough Avenue
Tampa, FL 33634
813-882-8635

Kodak Colorsqueeze
Kodak
343 State Street
Rochester, NY 14650
800-233-1650

New Fountain
David Blatner, Parallax Productions
5001 Ravenna Avenue N.E., Suite 13
Seattle, WA 98105

On Cue
Icom Simulations, Inc.
648 S. Wheeling Road
Wheeling, IL 60090
708-520-4440

Overwood 2.0, shareware
Jim Donnelly, College of Education
University of Maryland
College Park, MD 20742

Pyro!
Fifth Generation Systems, Inc.
10049 Reiger Road
Baton Rouge, LA 70809
800-873-4384

QuicKeys
CE Software
PO Box 65580
W. Des Moines, IA 50265
515-224-1995

Screen-to-PICT, public domain
Educorp
7434 Trade Street
San Diego, CA 92121
800-843-9497

SmartScrap
Solutions International
30 Commerce Street
Williston, VT 05495
802-658-5506

Suitcase II
Fifth Generation Systems
10049 N. Reiger Road
Baton Rouge, LA 70809
800-873-4384

Prepress Systems

Aldus PrePrint
Aldus Corporation
411 First Avenue S.
Seattle, WA 98104
206-622-5500

Crosfield
Crosfield Systems, Marketing Division
65 Harristown Road
Glen Rock, NJ 07452
201-447-5800, ext. 5310

Freedom of Press
Custom Applications, Inc.
900 Technology Park Drive, Bldg 8
Billerica, MA 01821
508-667-8585

Lightspeed Color Layout System
Lightspeed
47 Farnsworth Street
Boston, MA 02210
617-338-2173

Printware 720 IQ Laser Imager
Printware, Inc.
1385 Mendota Heights Road
Saint Paul, MN 55120
612-456-1400

SpectreSeps PM
Pre-Press Technologies, Inc.
2441 Impala Drive
Carlsbad, CA 92008
619-931-2695

Visionary
Scitex America Corporation
8 Oak Park Drive
Bedford, MA 01730
617-275-5150

Printers and Imagesetters

BirmySetter 300 & 400 Imagesetters
Birmy Graphics Corporation
PO Box 42-0591
Miami, FL 33142
305-633-3321

CG 9600/9700-PS Imagesetters
Agfa Compugraphic Corporation
90 Industrial Way
Wilmington, MA 01887
800-622-8973

Chelgraph A3 Imageprinter
Electra Products, Inc.
1 Survey Circle
N. Billerica, MA 01862
508-663-4366

Chelgraph IBX Imagesetter
Electra Products, Inc.
1 Survey Circle
N. Billerica, MA 01862
508-663-4366

ColorMate PostScript printer
NEC Technologies, Inc.
Printer Marketing Division
159 Swanson Road
Boxborough, MA 01719
800-632-4636

ColorPoint
Seiko Instruments
1130 Ringwood Ct.
San Jose, CA 95131
800-873-4561

ColorQuick
Tektronix, Inc.
Graphics Printing & Imaging Division
PO Box 500, M/S 50-662
Beaverton, OR 97077
503-627-1497

Colorsetter 2000
Optronics, An Intergraph Division
7 Stuart Road
Chelmsford, MA 01824
508-256-4511

Compugraphic Imagesetters
Agfa Compugraphic Corporation
200 Ballardvale Street
Wilmington, MA 01887
508-658-5600

4CAST
Du Pont Electronic Imaging Systems
300 Bellevue Parkway, Suite 390
Wilmington, DE 19809
800-654-4567

HP LaserJet Series II
Hewlett-Packard Company
PO Box 60008
Sunnyvale, CA 94088-60008
800-538-8787

HP PaintJet
Hewlett-Packard Company
PO Box 60008
Sunnyvale, CA 94088-60008
800-538-8787

ImageWriter II
Apple Computer, Inc.
20525 Mariani Avenue
Cupertino, CA 95014
408-996-1010

JLaser CR1
Tall Tree Systems
2585 Bayshore Road
Palo Alto, CA 94303
415-493-1980

Lasersmith PS-415 Laser Printers
Lasersmith, Inc.
430 Martin Avenue
Santa Clara, CA 95050
408-727-7700

LaserWriter II family of printers
Apple Computer, Inc.
20525 Mariani Avenue
Cupertino, CA 95014
408-996-1010

Linotronic imagesetters
Linotype Company
425 Oser Avenue
Hauppauge, NY 11788
516-434-2000

LZR Series Laser Printers
Dataproducts
6200 Canoga Avenue
Woodland Hills, CA 91365
818-887-8000

**Mitsubishi G330-70
color thermal printer**
Mitsubishi Electronics America
Computer Peripherals Products
991 Knox Street
Torrance, CA 90502
213-515-3993

Omnilaser Series 2000
Texas Instruments Inc.
12501 Research
Austin, TX 78769
512-250-7111

**Pacific Page
(PostScript emulation cartridge)**
Golden Eagle Micro, Inc.
8515 Zionsville Road
Indianapolis, IN 46268
317-879-9696

Phaser Color Image Printer
Tektronix, Inc.,
Graphics Printing & Imaging Division
PO Box 500, M/S 50-662
Beaverton, OR 97077
503-627-1497

QMS ColorScript printers
QMS, Inc.
1 Magnum Pass
Mobile, AL 36618
800-631-2693

QMS-PS Series Laser Printers
QMS, Inc.
1 Magnum Pass
Mobile, AL 36618
800-631-2693

Series 1000 Imagesetters
Linotype Company
4215 Oser Avenue
Hauppauge, NY 11788
516-434-2014

Turbo PS Series Laser Printer
NewGen Systems Corporation
17580 Newhope Street
Fountain Valley, CA 92708
714-641-2800

UltreSetter
Ultre Corporation
145 Pinelawn Road
Melville, NY 11747
516-753-4800

Varityper printers
Varityper, A Tegra Company
11 Mt. Pleasant Avenue
East Hanover, NJ 07936
201-884-6277

Large-Format Output Services

Computer Image Systems
20030 Normandie Avenue
Torrance, CA 90502
800-736-5105

Gamma One
12 Corporate Drive
North Haven, CT 06473
203-234-0440

Jetgraphix
1531 Pontus Avenue, Suite 300
Los Angeles, CA 90025
213-479-4994

Film Recorders

Agfa-Matrix Film Recorder
Agfa
1 Ramland Road
Orangeburg, NY 10962
914-365-0190

FilmPrinterPlus
Mirus
4301 Great America Parkway
Santa Clara, CA 95054
408-980-9770

Periodicals

Aldus magazine
Aldus Corporation
411 First Avenue S.
Seattle, WA 98104
206-622-5500

Colophon
Font & Function
Adobe Systems, Inc.
PO Box 7900
Mountain View, CA 94039-7900
800-344-8335

MacUser
PC magazine
Ziff-Davis Publishing Company
1 Park Avenue
New York, NY 10016
800-627-2247

Macworld
IDG Communications, Inc.
501 Second Street
San Francisco, CA 94107
800-234-1038

Personal Publishing
Hitchcock Publishing Company
191 S. Gary Avenue
Carol Stream, IL 60188
800-727-6937

Publish
PCW Communications, Inc.
501 Second Street
San Francisco, CA 94107
800-222-2990

Step-by-Step Electronic Design
Dynamic Graphics, Inc.
6000 N. Forest Park Drive
Peoria, IL 61614-3592
800-255-8800

U&lc
International Typeface Corporation
2 Hammarskjold Place
New York, NY 10017
212-371-0699

Verbum magazine
Verbum, Inc.
PO Box 15439
San Diego, CA 92115
619-233-9977

Books

The Gray Book
Ventana Press
PO Box 2468
Chapel Hill, NC 27515
919-942-0220

Making Art on the Macintosh II
Scott, Foresman and Company
1900 E. Lake Avenue
Glenview, IL 60025
312-729-3000

The Verbum Book of Digital Painting
M&T Books
501 Galveston Drive
Redwood City, CA 94063
415-366-3600

Bulletin Board Services

CompuServe Information Services, Inc.
5000 Arlington Center Boulevard
Columbus, OH 43260
800-848-8199

**Connect Professional
Information Network**
Connect, Inc.
10161 Bubb Road
Cupertino, CA 95014
408-973-0110

Desktop Express
Dow Jones & Company
Princeton, NJ 08543
609-520-4000

Genie
GE Information Services
401 N. Washington Street
Rockville, MD 20850
800-638-9636

MCI Mail
1150 17th Street N.W., Suite 800
Washington, DC 20036
800-444-6245

Communication Software

Microphone II
Software Ventures
2907 Claremont Avenue, Suite 220
Berkeley, CA 94705
800-336-6477

Red Ryder
Free Soft
150 Hickory Drive
Beaver Falls, PA 15010
412-846-2700

This book was designed and produced primarily on Macintoshes, although several other kinds of computer systems were used. Text was input primarily in Microsoft Word on a Macintosh IIci and a Mac Plus. Other computers used in design and production of the book included a Mac II, a second Macintosh IIci, a IIcx, an SE and a Plus.

Text files supplied by artists were converted, if necessary, to Microsoft Word format on the Mac. Files were checked with Word's Spelling function; the Change (search-and-replace) function was used to find and eliminate extra spaces and to insert *fi* and *fl* ligatures.

Pages were laid out and styled using PageMaker 4.0. Body text was set in Adobe's Galliard (10/14.5), and captions in Franklin Gothic (7/8). A Zapf Dingbats "z" was used for the "hint" symbol.

Illustrations for the project chapters and gallery were created as described in the text and in most cases were supplied by the artist as application files. Most artwork for the book and cover was saved in TIFF or PICT format and placed in the PageMaker files. Screen shots to show software interfaces were made on a Mac II using FKeys such as Command-Shift-6 (color screen clip), Command-Shift-7 (screen-to-PICT) or the Camera desk accessory on a Mac Plus. Color PICT files were imported into Adobe Photoshop for conversion to color TIFF files before being placed. All of the art in Chapter 8 was saved as Targa .TGA files on Macintosh-formatted floppies and then opened in Adobe Photoshop and saved as TIFF files for placement in the PageMaker document. Color TIFF files were saved with the LZW Compression option available in Photoshop to conserve disk space. Some grayscale images, for example the ones in Chapter 5, were saved as EPSF files. The "Verbum Electronic Art and Design Series" logo was created in FreeHand and placed as an EPS in the PageMaker file for the cover.

During final layout and production, files were stored on 45 MB removable cartridge drives. An Apple IINTX laser printer and a Tektronix Phaser color PostScript printer were used for proofing pages. Pages were output by Applied Graphics Technologies of Foster City, California on a Linotronic L-300 imagesetter with a RIP 3. Pages with type and line art only were output as negatives at 1270 dpi; pages with screen tints or grayscale images were output as negatives at 2540 dpi. Pages with embedded four-color graphics were separated using Aldus PrePrint and output as negatives at 2540 dpi. Central Graphics of San Diego also provided output services.

In some cases artwork was provided to Applied Graphics Technologies as 35mm transparencies or as final printed pieces, which were shot as halftones or color separated and stripped into the page negatives. Artwork from computer systems other than Macintosh were handled this way, for example.

Special thanks to Jack Davis for the illustrations in Chapters 1 and 2, and for all his technical and moral support.

S U B S C R I B E !

KEEP YOUR EDGE!

"The emergence of good taste... these guys are very serious about doing things right." – John Dvorak, PC Industry Analyst

CHANGE THE WORLD!

"If I were stranded on a desert island, this is the magazine I'd want with me" – Bob Roberts, *MIPS Journal*

"Artists are grabbing the cursor and spawning a distinct design sense, which this classy journal explores." – *Whole Earth Review*

GET RICH!

PUSH THE ENVELOPE!

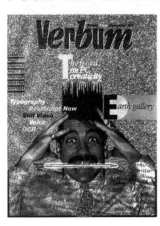

"I love your inspiring use of media...what should we call this? 'Magazine' hardly seems appropriate." – Chuck Pratt, subscriber, University of Texas

MULTI YOUR MEDIA!

THE JOURNAL OF PERSONAL COMPUTER AESTHETICS

Join the inner circle of electronic art, design and multimedia professionals who've counted on *Verbum* since 1986 to deliver the cutting edge: the Verbum Gallery, regular columns, feature stories, new products, ideas, insights — *synergy*. *Verbum* is both substance *and* style — each issue uses the latest tools and programs to push the limits of desktop publishing.

Verbum Stack 2.0
1990 version of the famous Verbum Stack with usable start-up screens and icons, as well as tons of great bitmap art, sounds, animations and surprises. Shipped on two 800k floppies.

Verbum **Digital Type Poster** Designed by Jack Davis and Susan Merritt, this deluxe 5-color, 17 x 22-inch poster showcases the variety of digital type effects possible on the Macintosh. Produced on a Mac II with PageMaker 3.0, output on a Linotronic L-300 and printed on a 100 lb. coated sheet. Text explains the history of initial caps in publishing, and how each sample letter was created. A framable "illuminated manuscript" for every electronic design studio! Limited edition of 2000. Shipped in capped tube.

Keep abreast of technology and creativity...

Subscribe to VERBUM, order back issues and products by filling in this user-friendly form and we'll keep you up-to-date on the latest in pc art and news!

Name _____   Organization _____

Address _____   Phone _____

City _____ State _____ ZIP _____ Country _____

☐ **ONE YEAR/4-ISSUE SUBSCRIPTION** – $24; Canada & Mexico – $36 US funds; all other countries – $45 US funds

☐ **TWO YEAR/8-ISSUE SUBSCRIPTION** – $46; Canada & Mexico – $72 US funds; all other countries – $90 US funds

☐ **BACK ISSUES** – $7 each: (circle issue/s)   1.1   1.2   1.3   2.1   2.3   3.1   3.2   3.3   3.4   4.1   4.2   4.3

☐ **VERBUM STACK 2.0** – $12 (includes lifetime registration for add-on releases)

☐ **VERBUM DIGITAL TYPE POSTER** – $10 (including tube and shipping)

TOTAL AMOUNT (plus $2.50 shipping for products and back issues) $_____
California residents please add 7¼% sales tax for products and back issues.

☐ **Check enclosed**

☐ **VISA/MC #** _____ exp _____

Send to: VERBUM, PO Box 12564, San Diego, CA 92112 or call 619/233-9977 with credit card number. Allow six weeks for delivery.

SI Book